Leslie Leland Locke

**The ideal new woman**

After real old models

Leslie Leland Locke

**The ideal new woman**
*After real old models*

ISBN/EAN: 9783741179310

Manufactured in Europe, USA, Canada, Australia, Japa

Cover: Foto ©Lupo / pixelio.de

Manufactured and distributed by brebook publishing software (www.brebook.com)

Leslie Leland Locke

**The ideal new woman**

# THE
# IDEAL NEW WOMAN

AFTER

## REAL OLD MODELS.

FROM THE FRENCH OF THE

COUNTESS ERNESTINE DE TRÉMAUDAN.

*By Permission of the Authoress.*

ST. LOUIS, MO. 1899.
Published by B. HERDER,
17 South Broadway.

NIHIL OBSTAT.

F. G. HOLWECK,
Censor Theologicus.

St. Louis, Sept. 23d, 1898.


IMPRIMATUR.

✢ JOHN J. KAIN,
Abp. of St. Louis.

St. Louis, Sept. 24th, 1898.

---

Copyright, 1899, by Joseph Gummersbach.

# CONTENTS.

|  |  | PAGE. |
|---|---|---|
|  | INTRODUCTION. | 3 |
| 1. | ELISABETH. | 11 |
| 2. | ANNA, THE PROPHETESS. | 23 |
| 3. | THE SAMARITAN WOMAN. | 33 |
| 4. | THE WIDOW OF NAIM. | 50 |
| 5. | THE WOMEN WHO SERVE JESUS. | 57 |
| 6. | THE WOMAN UNDER AN ISSUE OF BLOOD AND THE DAUGHTER OF JAIRUS. | 65 |
| 7. | MARY MAGDALEN PARDONED. | 75 |
| 8. | THE ADULTEROUS WOMAN. | 89 |
| 9. | JUSTA THE CANANEAN. | 101 |
| 10. | MARTHA AND MARY. | 110 |
| 11. | THE WOMAN UNDER A SPIRIT OF INFIRMITY. | 123 |
| 12. | THE RESURRECTION OF LAZARUS. | 136 |
| 13. | THE WIDOW'S MITE. | 150 |
| 14. | MARY MAGDALEN. | 158 |
| 15. | CLAUDIA PROCULA, WIFE OF PILATE. | 170 |
| 16. | WOMEN ACCOMPANY JESUS TO CALVARY. | 180 |
| 17. | THE WOMEN ON GOLGATHA. | 189 |
| 18. | MARY MAGDALEN AT THE TOMB OF JESUS. | 197 |
| 19. | THE WOMEN AT THE SEPULCHRE. | 207 |
| 20. | THE WOMEN AT THE CENACULUM. | 219 |

# INTRODUCTION.

REACTION has set in against the philosophic and wordly ideas of the XVIII. century, which demanded of woman to be cheerful and genial, but ignorant and frivolous, unconscious of her duties and rights, and without religion and morals.

This reaction is due to two opposing currents, one having its source in Free-thought and Masonry, the other, in the Gospel. Infidels, sectaries, and Christians rival with each other in the discussion of the very serious question of "Femininism"; journals, reviews, and books, preachers and legislators are busy about it. No one doubts any longer the intellectual aptitude of woman;\*) and

---

\*) "As Christianity shows, and every one of us knows, woman is a being neither superior nor inferior to man, endowed with faculties not less ample but different from his and in harmony with her physical nature, answering the end for which she is created. She may vindicate for herself the same rights as we, though under the essential reserve that they correspond with her providential mission."

Gabriel Alix, in *La Réforme Sociale* (Oct. 1896.)

whilst it is generally agreed that in many instances her instruction has been neglected and her legal position lowered, opinion is divided as to granting her all the rights of a legal voter.*)

---

*) "As early as 1871, Admiral de Gueydon, in his remarkable essay on "Political Equality," expressed himself thus: "Can one reasonably qualify as universal a suffrage that takes no notice of the interests of women and children? What becomes of the considerations of age and sex when there is question of taxes? They disappear: everybody has to pay. Hence everybody, without distinction of age or sex, ought to partake also in the election of those who impose the taxes.

"Justice and reason are a unit in reclaiming political equality on the same ground and by the very means by which each is assured the enjoyment of this equality before the civil law. It is thus in industrial, social, and commercial societies: no question is asked about the age or the sex of the member; a single interest is sufficient to secure the right of representation. It should be the same in the large society called the nation. Each having an interest in the good government of the State, each has a right to intervene directly or indirectly according to his capability."

M. Gabriel Alix wants to grant women a limited vote only:

"We are opposed to a single register, we demand an electoral register, which, besides the present legal voters, contains the names of women and minors as well as of all corporations and establishments of public utility discharging local affairs, for all municipal and provincial elections."

## Introduction. 5

In brief, the "feminine question" has become part of the "social question" to such an extent that, "to solve the former means to advance the solution of the latter."*)

Here we find the explanation why Socialists and Masons are so earnestly at work to draw women to their side. They are well aware that "the hand that rocks the cradle is the hand that rules the world."

"The foundations of the present order," writes the Socialist Bebel, "are undermined; the revolutionary spirit enters everywhere. Hence woman is not to remain inactive; she must consecrate her forces to whomsoever shall affranchise her together with the proletarian. With her assistance victory is ours." **)

At the "Free-thought Congress" of Sept. 19, 1881, the President thanked the members for having added a woman to the list of officers, saying: "On woman the Free-thinkers have placed their hope for the conversion of the future."

And the Congress of the French Federation of Free-thought (Nov. 1893) contained in

---

*) "The Feminine Question in Germany." By Mary André. *Correspondant* of March 10, 1896.

**) Bebel, "Socialism and Woman."

its declaration of principles the significant words: "The influence of Free-thought on the moral, economic, and social condition of woman forms part of our discussions as also the study of the most practical means to withdraw women from the disastrous influence of the priest."

Masonry expresses itself in the same terms as Socialism and Free-thought:

"We have accomplished nothing," they say, "as long as the women are not on our side; we must gain them for us: all men united avail nothing without them."

The French government eagerly lent itself to the service of these destructive ideas. It decreed the obligatory instruction of girls without the catechism and created for that purpose high schools without chaplains.*) Hand in hand with the high schools, the normal institutes for young ladies, the asylums, orphanages, and professional lay schools work at this dechristianization.

---

*) There are in France, according to M. C. Sée, one of the chief promoters of those iniquitous laws, 63 colleges for young ladies, having 800 professors and 10,413 pupils. The maintenance of these establishments annually requires 49,044,957 francs; on an average each pupil costs the tax payers, 4,710 francs = $816.20.

## Introduction. 7

But the bitter fruits of an atheistic education have not been slow to ripen; even Freethinkers lament in the high school graduates and other young ladies with diplomas the lack of a proper education, the crammed brains and cramped bodies, their superficial and false knowledge, their self-infatuation and chimerical conception of life, the dissatisfaction with their social position, their want of morality and restraint. The frightful increase of youthful criminality, misery and vice *) are a standing complaint of the daily press.

Not a small part of this criminality must be attributed to the overproduction of young ladies with diplomas.**)

Long ago the Saviour had said: "A bad tree cannot bear good fruit." Since man

---

*) "From 1880 to 1890 the number of young criminals increased one fourth, whilst the crimes of adults increased but one ninth. The criminality of the young is almost double that of the adults to-day." (Eug. Rostand, in *La Reforme Sociale* of March 1, 1897.

**) Of 30,000 breveted young ladies applying for office, but 3,000 obtained a situation with the government, and 2,000 more were promised an appointment as teachers within five years. 25,000, after much suffering, returned home, and 3,500 fell a prey to vice.

exists, the tree of knowledge has never borne wholesome fruit, except where planted in divine ground, watched and pruned by select gardeners. This law is absolute and without any exception. It concerns the education of both sexes; the soul of woman, in particular, owes its moral and intellectual redemption to Christianity.

The most famous philosophers of Greek and Roman antiquity never addressed themselves to women; when they had to speak of her, they did it with contempt and for her further degradation. But the Saviour instructed women and spoke to them of themselves; a great many of His actions were performed for her reformation and elevation. And no wonder: He knew they were indispensable cooperators in the salvation, both earthly and heavenly, of humanity.

Since the Saviour's ascension woman is transformed: at the Cenaculum, in the person of the Mother of God and that of the other holy women, she received the effusion of the Spirit of Wisdom, of Force, and of Charity; the Apostles associated her with them in the apostolate and speak of her assistance with respectful gratitude. In the Middle Ages, all Catholic nations, likewise, honored and even exalted her.\*)

And even later on, at the domestic hearth and in the life of the community, they assigned to her the place the Word of Redemption had indirectly given her.\*\*)

To show her this unheard-of and ever memorable blessing, to make her love and esteem the Saviour more for His grand intervention in favor of the "weaker sex," was our aim in composing this small volume. To Him alone she owes the Charter of her affranchisement in soul and body, in mind and will, in her private and public life; it was not granted her yesterday in the name of public opinion or "modern progress," neither by an assembly of legislators, nor a congress of

---

\*) Knighthood.

\*\*) As suzerain she coins money and renders justice; as juror she serves her corporation; as citizen she is called to the city councils and hospitals, in villages to the revision of local customs and laws. In short: as young lady, wife, or widow, woman represents the thing, i. e. the workingtool or shop or landed estate for the defense of whose interests she has the same rights as man. In 1576, 32 widows had a seat in the provincial council of the Franche Comté. Only by revolutionary and tyranical codes has the social standing of woman been curtailed or annihilated.

citizens. The God-Man, Who descended from Heaven to save all men from error and perdition, had also come to proclaim the equality of all before God. At a time when, by seductive sophisms and deceitful promises, woman's rights and mission are superexalted, as of yore in the garden ot Eden, it is of importance that Christian women attentively read and earnestly contemplate those passages of Holy Writ that concern them; that more than ever they carefully consider their duties and rights and the close and necessary relation binding them with the very destinies of Catholicity itself.

For that purpose we have gathered a number of texts from the Gospels and present them here as a summary of the calls which the Master addressed to the women-workers in His Church and as faint outline of woman's Redemption.

# ELISABETH.

## WOMAN, THE FIRST TO GLORIFY THE SAVIOUR.

ACHARY and Elisabeth, according to tradition, lived at Hebron, a town of Juda, situated on about the same altitude as Jerusalem and Bethlehem. Hebron, at present El Khabil, a name given it in memory of Abraham, signifying city of the Friend of God, is the last populous town towards the desert. Famous vineyards surround it. It dominates a valley which, at the time of our narrative, produced the choicest fruits of the whole land of Chanaan. As a sacerdotal town it was the abode of four of the ancient classes of priests who alternately performed the service in the Temple. Although forty-five miles away from Jerusalem, on bright days the pinnacles of the Temple were clearly visible from its elevation.

According to a more trustworthy tradition, Elisabeth received the visit of her holy cousin Mary at Ain-Karin. A chapel at that place is said to stand on the very spot where the salutation took place. When, in 1860, that chapel had fallen into ruins, and the Franciscan Fathers began to remove the debris, they discovered an oratory, formed partly by the rock, partly by the strong walls on which another sanctuary rested. These two rooms, one on top of the other, are called by the natives Mar-Zacharia, and are said to have been part of the country residence of Zachary and Elisabeth. In the lower room took place the touching scene we call the Visitation.

In the neighborhood there is a monumental fountain, called the "Fountain of the Virgin," where the Mother of God used to draw water during her stay with Elisabeth. "Numerous Arabs", says the author of "*La Caravanne Française*," "perform there the customary ablutions, accompanied by the usual prostrations. Whilst they are thus occupied, the noise of our voices or of the horses will not even make them turn their heads. How earnest is the prayer of these people, and what a lesson for our levity!"

Another fact, absolutely true, because taught by Holy Scripture, is the descent of Zachary and Elisabeth from the family of Abia, who, when David divided the posterity of Aaron into twenty-four classes, obtained by lot the eighth rank in the service of the Temple.

When writing a biography, it is proper first to consider the hero's ancestry. If soil and climate and language act upon each individual, the influence of one's ancestors is not less considerable; for the law of intellectual and moral heredity is perhaps more real than that of physical heredity. Thus the transmission of religious tendencies is frequently observed, and the proverb says: "Saints are born of saints." Hence, nothing can be more desirable than a union of persons equally near and dear to God.

Such was the union of Zachary and Elisabeth. "Both," says Holy Scripture, "were just before God." *) By conscientiously keeping the commandments of the Lord, they set an example of that beautiful conjugal life which has its root in the love of God and fidelity to His laws. "To be just," to walk

---
*) Luke I.

in the commandments, how many noble ideas are contained in these words!

Zachary and Elisabeth had not set their hearts on riches, nor did they seek pleasures and honors, objects of vulgar activity, baits for ordinary mortals. Their souls' aim was higher: they practiced justice towards God and man. God was the center of all their thoughts, the sole object of their ambition and love.

They lived together — models of conjugal life as God wills it. Mutual assistance in marriage presupposes a proper understanding of the respect, confidence, and tenderness due to one another; it means a mutual completion by an exchange of force and grace, intelligence and sentiment, and, above all, of virtues.

Mutual help in marriage means to share the joys and sorrows of life; but it often also means to sacrifice one's own tastes and inclinations and personal opinions, which cannot and will not be done, unless both husband and wife have the same faith and their eyes fixed on Heaven.

Zachary and Elisabeth enjoyed this happiness, but lacked another, that of offspring. Their days passed in sadness. The Jewish people did not know the selfish practice which, in our days, is the grave of affection and all family virtues, and a menace to the population of earth and Heaven. For a people that had to fill the land of Chanaan and to conquer the enemies of Jehova, to "increase and multiply" was both a religious and a national duty. Numerous children where considered an honor to the family and a celestial and terrestrial blessing. The glorious hope, moreover, of giving Israel its Messiah, increased in women the longing after motherhood. Besides, as under the Old Law woman had no personality, it was but natural that she should seek and find her happiness in the bosom of the family. To Christianity alone does she owe her religious and social individuality.

Zachary and Elisabeth, advanced in age, had given up all hope. What sadness and humiliation for their old days! But the very best are not spared trials — sure signs of God's predilection, which, if borne patiently, are frequently rewarded already on earth.

"And it came to pass, when he executed the priestly functions in the order of his course before God, according to the custom of his priestly office, it was his lot to offer incense, going into the temple of the Lord; and all the people were praying without at the hour of incense. And there appeared to him an angel of the Lord, standing on the right side of the altar of incense. And Zachary seeing him was troubled and fear fell upon him. But the angel said to him: 'Fear not, Zachary, for thy prayer is heard; and thy wife Elisabeth shall bear thee a son, and thou shalt call his name John.' "

Zachary, doubting this promise, was struck dumb. Meanwhile the promise is realized; and Elisabeth, hiding her motherhood for five months, incessantly praised and thanked God in fervent prayers; "for He has taken away my humiliation in the sight of men."

The example of recollection given by Elisabeth is followed by all Christian mothers who deserve that God may say of their offspring: "Before thou wast born, I already had chosen and predestined thee." This grace of recollection, so full of interior joys, is the fruit of ardent prayers, careful avoidance of all evil, and of the continuous practice of good.

You are right, Elisabeth, enjoy your happiness in solitude and silence, give vent to it in thanksgiving! Thanksgiving is the rich source of many other favors. So far you enjoy but Heaven's first gift, the fruit of your prayers, another is in store for you as the reward of your faith. Zachary saw the angel at the right of the altar, but would not believe in the promised happiness; you, a firm believer, shall be honored by a higher presence.

"And Mary rising up in those days, went into the hill country with haste into the city of Juda." Since her marriage to Joseph, Mary lived in Nazareth, a small village in the fertile district of Galilee, crowned by the shady mountains of Libanon, whence the undulating valleys start that unite in the plain of Esdrelon. This plain, laid out in orchards and fields, forms a vast basin at one side of Nazareth, whilst on the other side it is protected by a row of hills, studded with poplar and fig trees and covered with rose-mallows.

This attractive and peaceful village Mary resolved to leave for a while, and pay a visit to her cousin Elisabeth in the hill country, east of the Dead Sea and north of the Arabian desert, a distance of about seventy miles.

The tender Virgin is neither dismayed by the hardships of such a trip, nor does she think for a moment that she, as the chosen Mother of God, should rather be visited and congratulated by Elisabeth. Her intelligent goodness makes her feel how it behooves the most exalted to go down to those who move on a lower level, and gives her the conviction that to make another happy is worth a little fatigue. Moreover, family connections ought to be kept up, and it is part of our religious duty to help our relatives. This cheerful visit of the Blessed Virgin appeared so beautiful to St. Francis of Sales that he gave the name of the Visitation to the congregation of women he founded.

The trip was long and wearisome, but the young traveler has stood it. Behold her enter the house of Elisabeth. The cousins know each other from former visits. They embrace one another, and there, in the presence of the Word Incarnate, fallen humanity, in the person of Elisabeth, feels a thrill of joy and entones that canticle of hope and redemption: "Blessed art thou among women, and blessed is the fruit of thy womb." At these words of Elisabeth, Mary, too, realizes her happiness, but she soars higher—through the clouds to the Giver—and exclaims:

"My soul does magnify the Lord: and my spirit hath rejoiced in God, my Saviour. Because he hath regarded the humility of His handmaid; for, behold, from henceforth all generations shall call me blessed."

By divine inspiration, Elisabeth knew the mystery of the Incarnation. A woman, a mother, is the first on earth to whom is revealed what even St. Joseph*) hitherto knew not—the conception of Him to Whom her child was to be the precursor. A woman with the promises of motherhood is the first to be visited by the Saviour in the womb of Mary, because in the son of this woman He wants to bless the entire race, poor humanity, for so many centuries astray from its God. John is sanctified by Jesus; for, "when Elisabeth heard the salutation of Mary, the infant leaped in her womb. And Elisabeth was filled with the Holy Ghost."

Thus Christ is our salvation, and by Mary,

---

*) "It was after the Visitation that Joseph resolved to send away Mary." (Ludolph, the Carthusian, in his large Life of Jesus Christ.)

the Mother of the Redeemer, we have received it.

And as John owes the privilege of being sanctified before his birth to the faith and piety of Elisabeth, so children, in general, owe their spiritual regeneration, the conservation and development of their supernatural life, to the faith of their mother and the care she takes to present them for baptism and instruct them in piety. Blessed, therefore, those mothers who by the most intimate visits of Jesus in Holy Communion, and by a life of piety and recollection at home, obtain the Saviour's blessing for their children during their mysterious sleep. Blessed are they who are firmly convinced that in Him alone is to be found the salvation of mother and child, the virtuous and happy future of humanity. Blessed those mothers who, from the first moment, resolve to co-operate with the intimate designs of God regarding their offspring's infancy and youth.

Mothers, never forget that the highest reason for congratulating you is that you gave birth to brothers of Jesus and citizens of Heaven.

For three months Mary and Jesus were the

guests of Elisabeth, for three months the infant Saviour kept on sanctifying his infant precursor.

Did the mothers know the fate awaiting their children: that the Son of the Eternal Father was to die by the cross? that the other, the penitent of the desert, was to be beheaded? It is believed the Blessed Virgin knew it, not so Elisabeth. Only the Queen of Martyrs is strong enough to bear such a continuous martyrdom. It was good for Elisabeth not to know the future. One Herod massacred her husband, another beheaded St. John. She herself was to die far away from her son.

The visits of the Lord mark His saints for adversity.

When the family presses eagerly around the cradle of the new-born babe, and the face of the mother is radiant with joy, as that of Elisabeth at the birth of John, the question is repeated for the thousandth time: "What a one, think ye, shall this child be?" The fond father and many others will predict a future of glory, yet God, invisibly present, answers: "Destined to suffer."

Lord, the more Thou lovest, the more Thy love presages sorrow!"

Your children, mothers, are destined to suffer. Train them for it. Teach them how to suffer in faith, in love, in watchfulness and patience, and they will be happy in the very midst of misery!

# ANNA, THE PROPHETESS.

### WOMAN ANNOUNCES THE SAVIOUR.

POETIC tradition tells us of a family that, travelling to Jerusalem, made halt under a terebinth whose branches bowed to greet, and spread to protect, its guests.\*) "I have stretched out my branches as a turpentine-tree, and my branches are of honor and grace."\*\*) Unknown and of humble appearance, this family, before which nature showed its reverence and which the whole world shall call the Holy Family, was on its journey to the Temple, there to fulfil the law.

---

\*) In later times the tree was honored even by Mohamedans.

\*\*) Eccli. XXIV. 22.

"I will move all nations," said the Prophet Aggeus, "and the Desired of all nations shall come: and I will fill this house with glory: saith the Lord of Hosts."

"Great shall be the glory of this last house more than that of the first, saith the Lord of Hosts: and in this place I will give peace, saith the Lord of Hosts." *)

The Temple to be honored for the first time by the presence of the Messiah was not the costly edifice of Solomon; it was the second Temple built by Zorobabel, plundered and almost destroyed by Crassus, profaned by Antiochus, but purified and reconsecrated by Judas Macchabeus. It had just been ornamented with royal munificence by Herod the Great and thus was ready to receive the "King of Israel" and the "Expected of the Nations." There the Messiah is to be presented to the Lord. Jerusalem rejoice, thy King approaches on the arms of His mother. "Lift up your gates, O ye princes, and be ye lifted up, O eternal gates: and the King of Glory shall enter in. Who is this King of Glory? The Lord of Hosts, He is the King of Glory." **)

---
*) Agg. II. 8—10.
**) Ps. XIII. 9, 10.

Mary waited at the gate of Nicanor, on the eastern side of the Temple, to be received with the sprinkling of blood by the priest, according to the Law of Moses. The altar is prepared for the redemption of the firstborn. As prescribed by the Law, the divine Mother deposits her gifts of the poor: fruits, two pigeons, and five shekels (about 25c). The infant is placed on the altar of the presentation. Clouds of incense and prayers ascend to Heaven, while one of the priests, taking up the new-born, lifts it toward the four sides of the Temple.

Mary, at the same time, offers to God her divine Son and the entire human race redeemed by Him. To woman was reserved this privilege of rendering to God, through God Himself, this first act of worship, alone worthy of Him. "I saw the Temple filled with glory, the brightness of which cannot be described," says Catherine of Emmerich in her Life of the Blessed Virgin. "I saw that God was present there; and above the Child I saw the Heavens open unto the throne of the most holy Trinity."

Apparently there is nothing to reveal these wonders, nothing that differs from other presentations, nothing that attracts the curiosity of the multitude. Silence reigns within the Temple, and in the city is the usual noise and din of vehicles and occupations. Greed of riches, pleasure or sorrow fill its inhabitants. Nothing unusual interrupts the ordinary run of men or affairs; yet an oblation of greatest importance to all mankind is to be made this very moment.

However, there are always scattered here and there some choice souls who share the secrets of Heaven and perceive what no one else does notice. Ordinarily living in solitude and recollection, they avoid the very shadow of evil and are ever attentive to the inspirations of the Holy Ghost. "O Father... Thou hast hid those things from the wise and prudent, and hast revealed them to little ones." *)

Now, there was in Jerusalem a man named Simeon, and this man was just and devout. And he came by the Spirit into the Temple. Recognizing in the child of the poor woman the promised Messiah, he takes Him on his arms and intones the ever beautiful canticle: "Now Thou dost dismiss Thy servant, O Lord,

---

*) Matt. XI. 25.

in peace, because my eyes have seen Thy salvation;" and, filled with the visions of the future, he predicts that this child will be "the light of the gentiles and the glory of His people Israel.".

And as if to confirm this prophecy and to complete it, as if to announce the good news to both sexes, to all minds and hearts, a prophetess arrives there likewise. Like Simeon, Anna is led to the Temple by the Holy Ghost. To her, too, the Incarnate Word makes Himself known as a weak and helpless child. With rapture Anna contemplates Him, takes Him in her arms, and puts her lips to His forehead, the seat of Divinity. Bliss and gratitude of these two old people, you enrapture mankind at its first contact with the Word Incarnate!

Now that he has seen the God Whom he has loved so much, Simeon has no other wish but to die. To die? ... Anna, is that your wish also? No, you have to live, to "speak of Him to all who are waiting for the redemption of Israel." In you, womankind, oppressed and trodden under foot by the civilization of antiquity, is to raise its voice and announce its redemption. Joel had foretold it: "And it shall come to pass after this, that I will pour out my spirit upon all flesh: and your sons and your daughters shall prophesy." *)

Anna was not the first woman on which the Spirit of the Lord had descended. Mary, the sister of Moses, Anna, the mother of Samuel, Judith and Deborah, Jahel and Esther, Elisabeth and, lastly, Mary, had spoken and acted in the name of the Lord. As a precursor to the Precursor, as an apostle to the Apostles, Anna had a mission of her own, that deserves to be studied by Christian women — she personifies their social and religious action.

The decadence of the Jewish people, predicted "for the last days" by the prophets Aggeus and Micheas, had arrived. Love for heathen festivals, ambition and jealousy, corruption in the priesthood, divisions and uproar among the citizens, present the spectacle of a nation that is dying in the pursuit of material pleasures. Misery reached its climax when Pompey, called to the aid of the sons of Janneus, reduced the land of the Jews to a Roman province. Herod the Idumean is appointed king of the Jews by the Roman

---
*) Joel II. 28.

senate. Whilst he oppresses the rich and influential families of the nation and deprives the Sanhedrin of its liberty and authority, in order to put his creatures in the office of the high priest: the Pharisees, self-constituted interpreters of the Law, oppress the common people and subject it to a multitude of superstitious practices that lead to indifference and irreligion.

In the midst of this political and religious corruption, Anna speaks of the Messiah to all who were waiting for the redemption of Israel. To indicate the importance of her mission, the Gospel speaks of her origin and her past life. She was the daughter of Phanuel, of the tribe of Aser. She had been married quite young, as is the custom in the Orient, but death had solved the union and shattered her earthly hopes. Then God had called her to His service in the Temple. There she had grown old in labors and watchings. It had not been without struggles and interior sufferings that she had broken with all that charms and captivates us here below, in order to lead a life of solitude, of prayer, and of penance; but as a just reward for her sacrifices, her soul is ennobled and elevated.

Anna lived in that part of the Temple which was exclusively reserved for women. Through one gate they could enter the enclosure of the Temple, through another, the streets of Jerusalem. There, at the expense of the Temple, were also raised the children that were to be consecrated to the Lord. The young girls were confided to the care of pious and considerate matrons, who instructed them in the Law and the Sacred Writings, taught them the psalms and prayers, and gave them lessons in manual labor for the service of the Temple.

Jewish history tells us that, at all times, women were employed for the service of the altar, and lived in the neighborhood of the Lord's House.

Thus, according to tradition, Anna, the prophetess, together with Noemi, had the charge of raising and instructing that child of divine predilection who called herself Mary of Nazareth. At the age of three years, Mary had been brought to the Temple by Anna, her mother, and Joachim, her father, and consecrated to the Lord. Did the prophetess ever penetrate into the destiny of that child and enjoy the previous knowledge that she was to be the mother of the Saviour? We do not know; but we do know that, by the study of the Law and the sanctity of her life, she deserved to behold the infant Saviour and glorify Him.

The apostolate is fruitful only when it deserves it. We cannot benefit the souls of others when we are without recollection and purity, when we do not try to instruct ourselves properly in the teachings of our holy religion, when we do not take proper care of our own house, another temple, in which God dwells within. It is not enough to speak of religion, to deplore the evils of our times, to arm ourselves with good principles: the Lord wants apostles that truly know Him and, by their lives, truly resemble Him. Worldlings He abandons to their worldly glory, to their false successes. To announce Himself He chose, not princes, not the priests of Israel, not the rich, but an humble woman, living in solitude and occupied with God.

The Gospel, likewise, says that only those who waited for the redemption of Israel were favored with the good news of His coming. The teaching of truth, to be efficacious, must be done opportunely. Anna knew the time to be silent, and the time to speak. Multiplying words, without discretion, at wrong moments, may lead away from faith and Christian practice those whom we wish to bring there.

The Gospel is silent about Anna's last days on earth. There is no need of words, either. She recognized the infant Saviour, she announced Him, she loved Him — to possess Him eternally in Heaven.

# THE SAMARITAN WOMAN.

### WOMAN POINTS OUT THE MESSIAH AND SHOWS THE WAY TO HIM.

THIRTY years of hidden life, years of labor and privation, Jesus had passed in the bosom of the Holy Family without attracting any particular notice. The Precursor was now proclaiming aloud the coming of the Messiah. Immense crowds flocked around him, attracted by the novelty of his preaching and the strangeness of his life. It was the hour of general expectation that every breath of air increased. Jesus Himself mingled with the crowds and went to be baptized by John and to recognize the high mission of the Hermit. Who, then, at this hour of wonders, should pay any attention to the Son of the carpenter of Nazareth?

Nevertheless, this condescension of Jesus to be baptized by John marked the end of His hidden life. Recognized and pointed out to the multitudes as the Messiah by John himself, the Saviour begins His journey through Palestine.

He was now in His thirty-first year and had just celebrated the first Easter after His baptism at Jerusalem. On his return to Galilee He took the ordinary route through Samaria and stopped at a village called Sichar or Sichem, now Naplous.

There the pilgrims, in spite of their traditional hatred against the Samaritans, passed their first night. The Samaritan people, descended from Assyrian tribes, had taken possession of the land of Ephraim during the Babylonian captivity and had founded the city of Samaria, which later on gave its name to the whole province. However, at the time of Jesus, Sichem had become its capital. Sichem was situated at the foot of Mount Hebal and Mount Garizim, in the deep valey of Samaria, "that grand thoroughfare under the sky of the setting sun, made as it were to give passage to the word of Christ towards the lands of the Occident, where it has brought the life." (P. Didon.)

Even to-day, nothwithstanding its ruins and the sadness hanging over this part of Palestine, Naplous, the ancient Sichem, is comparatively prosperous. Situated on the great route from Jerusalem to Damascus, at the parting of the valleys that descend west towards the Mediteranean and east towards the Jordan, it has an abundant water supply, that surrounds it with a green belt of gardens and vineyards.

This was the favorite dwelling place of the Patriarchs, rich in souvenirs: Abraham had stopped there when he had arrived in the "Land of Promise," and, under the oaktrees of Moreh (Mambre) he erected an altar to the Lord upon his return from Mesopotamia. Jacob, too, had erected an altar there to Jehova, and had bought from the sons of Hemor a field for his son Joseph, who turned it into a burial place; the Hebrews, surrounding the Ark after the passage through the Jordan, received there the blessing of Joshua;

there also, not far from the well of Jacob, the ancients of Israel reposed in their final resting places.

At this point of the road, "Jesus being wearied with his journey, sat on the well, about the sixth hour," *) *i. e.*, noon, and rested. His disciples, meanwhile, went to Sichem to provide victuals. Whilst He was thus alone, a Samaritan woman, carrying a jug on her shoulder, in the proud attitude of her race, arrived there, alone, contrary to custom; for, ordinarily, the women of the Orient come in groups, and towards evening, to draw water. She at once recognized the stranger and the Jew in the traveler. From indifference or haughtines, she had no salute for him. What cared she for the unknown, who, probably, despised her, like the rest of his nation, or even hated her. She is mistaken. The Stranger, apparently resting from the fatigue of His journey, in reality, is intent upon saving her soul. Hence, He begins to speak to her.

Thus, at the beginning of His public life, the Messiah addresses Himself to a woman. Woman, in the fall of the race the more

---
*) John IV.

guilty, and, since then, oppressed the world over, has special claims to redemption. But Jesus addresses her also, to make of her a powerful ally for the renewal of the world. He knows her domestic and social importance, and what treasures of devotion and love she can consecrate to her Saviour.

Yet, before He begins His instruction, He wants to put Himself under obligation to her. Hence, He says to her: "Give me to drink."

This demand, in itself, was very natural. Under a burning sky, the first duty of hospitality is to offer a drink to the traveler; but here the demand was made for a higher reason. Jesus, knowing the human heart, knows, too, that nothing will attach it so much as a service rendered.

The woman is surprised. What? An enemy of her nation, a Jew who, under severest penalties, is forbidden to eat or drink with the Samaritans, can he have anything to say to her?

She cannot hide her astonishment.

"How dost thou, being a Jew, ask of me to drink, who am a Samaritan woman?"

"Jesus answered and said to her: If thou didst know the gift of God, and who he is that says to thee, Give me to drink, thou perhaps wouldst have asked of him and he would have given thee living water." *)

This request of the Saviour is repeated to us daily: "God longs to be longed for."

"The woman saith to him: Sir, thou hast nothing wherein to draw, and the well is deep, from whence then hast thou living water? Art thou greater than our father Jacob, who gave us the well, and drank thereof himself, and his children, and his cattle?"

The woman has not understood the divine meaning; she can think but of perishable water; but she wishes to understand, and her words manifest both the training she has received by religious and social traditions, and the respect for her ancestors, who have left to this place their living history. "Forgetfulness and contempt of the past," says Guizot, "is a serious disorder and weakens a nation."

"Art thou greater than our father Jacob?"

"Jesus answered and said to her: Whoever

---

*) At this moment, the dream of Plato, of drinking at the source of Being and Truth, is realized for the Samaritan woman.

drinketh of this water shall thirst again, but he that shall drink of the water I will give him, shall not thirst forever; but the water that I will give him, shall become in him a fountain of water, springing up into life everlasting.''

The astonishment of Photina—thus tradition calls her — grows as her interlocutor speaks to her, but, as yet, she does not understand.

"The woman said to him, give me this water, that I may not thirst, nor come hither to draw.''

Little by little, Jesus had disposed her to address this demand to Him. So it frequently happens: God often speaks to a soul for a long time, without being understood, and, at times, He is quite near without being perceived.

"Go, call thy husband.'' The woman answers: "I have no husband.'' — "Thou hast said well: I have no husband. For thou hast had five husbands: and he, whom thou hast now, is not thy husband. This thou hast said truly.''

That settled it. Jesus had touched a sensible spot in her. With the art of His exquisite goodness, He has provoked the demand she addressed to Him for the mysterious water; He made her look upon Him as a superior man, greater than her fathers. These divine touches can hardly be perceived, so delicate they are, but how efficacious!

Jesus, Thou art wonderful in the art of touching souls! Thou knowest the sore of this woman, Thou art not ignorant of her interior shame and her secret sorrow, and now, continuing in the same simple strain, with the same goodness, Thou letst her hear the humiliating revelation of her life's faults. If Thou layest them bare before her eyes, Thou doest it to establish Thy divine mission and also to forgive them.

The woman is upright and sincere. To the joy of the Saviour, she does not try to deny, not even to excuse, them.

"The woman said to him: Sir, I perceive that thou art a prophet."

Still more astonished, still more subdued by respect, she gives this new title to Him Who penetrates her life. She suspicions even more; for, according to her co-religionists, one of the qualities of the Messiah consists in divining the most hidden thoughts.

Convinced that this man, at least, has a divine mission, she opens the serious question of the true religion.

"Our fathers adored on this mountain, and you say at Jerusalem is the place where men must adore."

Thus the Samaritan woman goes straight to the main affair of life, she puts the question, the answer to which is desired by every intelligent soul: What is the religious truth? How must we serve God? For such is essentially the question asked by her in such peculiar form: What solution dost thou give to the difficulty that separates Samaritans and Jews? Must we adore on this mountain or at Jerusalem?

Though leading a bad life, this woman had kept the spirit of religion and a certain interest in the eternal problems. Jesus leads her back to the truth by the exercise of her mind, her personal efforts, and prayer.

Fatigued as He is, He does not shorten the conversation; He does not weary instructing this attentive soul; every one of His words manifests loving goodness and the most encouraging interest.

"Woman, believe me," said He, "that the

hour cometh, when you shall neither on this mountain, nor in Jerusalem adore the Father."

"Believe me"—this word so often invoked by the impotence of our language, on the lips of the Eternal Word, possesses the power of commanding persuasion. And to widen the views of the Samaritan woman, while yet insisting on the first rights of Israel, Jesus proclaims the entrance of all men into the fold of the new alliance.

"You adore that which you know not, we adore that which we know; for salvation is of the Jews. But the hour cometh, and now is, when the true adorers shall adore the Father in spirit and in truth."

In view of the ignorance in which woman, considered by all peoples as inferior in rank, was kept all along, this teaching which Jesus gave her marks the beginning of her rehabilitation. This colloquy manifests the intellectual charity that seeks, instructs, and encourages those who are ignorant of, or combat, religious truth,— a rare charity, compared to the other that busies itself with the corporal works of mercy, since but few understand in what it consists, and how it should be practiced.

The astonishment of the woman becomes extreme, when Jesus tells her that God wishes to be honored by the mind, the will, and the heart, rather than by certain outward formulas and ceremonies. Bending one's knee in the church, reciting certain prayers, fulfilling the legal prescriptions, cannot satisfy God, when we offend Him wilfully or our heart is far from Him. Outward worship should be the manifestation of the inward sentiments. That is the true religion which inspires the whole life, which sacrifices to God all selfishness and pride. Man, indeed, can bring no better sacrifice than when he gives up his evil inclinations, can make no more pleasing offering than when he gives all his love to God.

"For the Father also seeketh such to adore Him."

Yes, God is constantly on the look-out for souls of good will, to pour into them His blessings and His glory. And to penetrate the Samaritan woman more deeply with the mystery of love, He insists and repeats:

"God is a spirit, and they that adore Him, must adore Him in spirit and in truth."

"In spirit": refined and detached from the

senses, nay from our very self. "In truth:" the return of the soul from the creature to God must be real; "we must detest that piety which consists in words only and love that which is solid, effective, and practical." (Bossuet.)

"*The woman saith to him: I know that the Messiah cometh (who is called Christ): therefore when he is come he will tell us all things.*"

She has as clear an understanding on this point as the most renowned philosophers, teaching that a God is needed to initiate man into the things pertaining to God. She, too, asserts that the Messiah of God is needed to save mankind; but besides, she believes he will not delay; she calls for him with all her heart. Such a disposition deserves a supreme grace. God always ends by showing Himself to those that seek Him. Jesus says to her:

"*I am he, who am speaking with thee.*"

To no one as yet had Jesus revealed Himself thus: the shepherds, and the Wise Men had adored Him as the "Promised One," "the one to be sent"; Elisabeth, Simeon, Anna, John the Baptist, Andrew and Philip had recognized Him as the Saviour of Israel; a voice from Heaven had proclaimed Him the Son of God;—but here, for the first time, and that to a woman, Jesus utters these solemn words:

"*I that speaks to thee, I am the Messiah.*"

"And immediately His disciples came and they wondered that He talked with the woman. Yet no man said: what seekest thou, or what talkest thou with her?"

A doctor of the Law, a prophet, speaking with a woman! And that woman not even a daughter of Abraham, but a Samaritan, a heretic. "Rather burn the words of the Law than lose time by teaching them to women," was a rabbinic saying, by which they wished to express, that woman was not capable of any deep religious training. A father in those days would have thought it contrary to common sense to instruct his daughter in the Law. Jewish customs had made this prejudice still stronger: a man dared not speak to a woman in public, nor ever salute her, and as the disciples had scarcely entered the school of Jesus, they still shared in full these notions of their countrymen.

Meanwhile, the woman had left her jug at

the well and had gone to the city, and said to the men there: "Come and see a man who has told me all things whatsoever I have done. Is not he the Christ?"

Moved by zeal, she speaks without fear of malevolent sneers, and braves the sarcastic remarks about her past life, in order to bring her compatriots to Jesus. What she told went from mouth to mouth, Sichem was filled with commotion.

"Now of that city many of the inhabitants believed in him, for the word of the woman giving testimony: He has told me all things whatsoever I have done."

Not the disciples, sent by Jesus into the town, make Him known there, but a woman had become His apostle; she announces to the Sichemites that the Messiah is quite near and expects them; and she leads them to Him. The privilege of initiating men in the faith is given her. She shall keep it forever. She shall, henceforth, fulfil this sacred duty in all stations of life: presenting the babe for baptism, teaching the child its prayers, speaking of God to the husband that ignores Him, to a brother or son that has strayed away from Him, to all who have forgotten

Him; placing the crucifix in the hand of the dying, holding it to his feeble lips to kiss it, reciting the last prayers with him and over him: — without ceasing she is to be the auxiliary of God; God has willed it thus.

"So when the Samaritans had come to him, they desired him to tarry there. And he abode there two days, and many more believed in him because of his own word."

Accepting the word of the woman, they themselves wish to see Jesus and to be instructed by Him. They leave their business to find Him. Thus, the child, instructed first by its mother in the rudiments of religion, must not stay in the catechism of the infancy, but approach the Saviour himself, and, by personal efforts, study and cultivate His manly spirit. To know God more and more is the object of all our life.

Had the Sichemites despised the appeal of the woman, they might have had but a vaccillating faith and have kept but a vague memory of the Saviour's visit. But whoever has seen Him, wants to see Him again and will hardly consent to His departure. Such a hold does He gain on our hearts.

"Stay with us," said the Sichemites, as

later on did the disciples at Emmaus. And He stayed. Two entire days the Redeemer deigned to spend with these heretics,\*) these despised people, that blended the cult of their false deities with that of Jehova. But among them were just souls, so that "many believed in him."

Then they said to the woman with a kind of pride: "We now believe, not for thy saying, for we ourselves have heard him and know that this is indeed the Saviour of the world."

She had wished nothing better. Happy the woman who, after having been instrumental to a divine work, can rejoice in gratitude to God and in her own nothingness in the eyes of men.

The ordinary mission of woman is not in public life, not in legislative or political meetings. When she has done her work at home and in its surroundings, when she has instructed, helped, and consoled those about her and spread some joy among them, she

---

\*) The Samaritans rejected all Sacred Writings, except the Books of Moses; but what they learned from them about the true God was grossly blended with their Assyrian theogony. Hence the Jews had no intercourse with them, as they were real heretics.

has announced Christ perfectly. Possibly those who were benefitted: her parents, children, husband, or others, think but little of her devotion or make light of her good actions, but God will never: He will take a correct account of them all and be Himself their "reward exceeding great." *)

---

*) According to tradition, the Samaritan woman received an exceptional mission: not only did she preach Christ in Samaria, but, like the Apostles, she went to distant shores. Under the reign of Nero she went to Africa with one of her sons to convert the city of Carthage. Brought back to Rome by order of Nero, she was martyred, together with her sons and sisters. She is venerated under the name of Photina. The Bollandists and the Roman and Greek Martyrologies give her feast on March 20th. The head of St. Photina, according to Baronius, is kept at Rome in the Basilica of St. Paul by the Benedictins of Monte Cassino.

# THE WIDOW OF NAIM.

NAIM, "the Beautiful", called thus on account of its attractive surroundings, at the time of Jesus was a prosperous and important city located at the extremity of Galilee, some hours walk from Nazareth near the sources of the Cison on the incline of the Little Hermon. Its high elevation offered an extensive and beautiful view of the neighborhood: on one side the hills of Nazareth, on the other, those of Carmel, and in the rear Mount Thabor. To-day we find but ruins and a few huts there. The tombs sunk into the rock on the eastern side are still fairly well preserved.

It was evening; a light fog covered the hillsides, the last rays of the sun gilt the clouds. Of the city, its walls and gates and dusty roads, but hazy outlines were visible. Jesus, surrounded by His disciples and followed by a noisy, curious crowd, eager to hear the words and see the deeds of the "great prophet," had arrived in its neighborhood.

"And when he came nigh to the gate of the city, behold a dead man was carried out, the only son of his mother; and she was a widow; and a great multitude of the city was with her." *)

After the custom of the Orient, the funeral cortege advanced slowly: at its head were the flute players; then came the men, their heads partly covered with their mantles, their feet bare, their vestments torn; then followed the bier with the dead youth, rapt in winding sheets; next came the mother and the other women, as also the hired mourners, who filled the air with lamentations and praises of the dead and alternately touched the tamburin to accompany the flute players.

Jesus met the funeral procession; He intended that meeting: He wished to witness one of woman's greatest sorrows, to behold with His own eyes the agonizing tears of a

---
*) Luke, VII. 12 seq.

mother. This widow, losing her son, lost her all and had no one left with whom she might seek consolation in weeping. The sadness and humiliation inflicted upon women by the ideas and customs of those days, were increased in her case, she being without protection and hope of posterity.

O woman, bereft of husband and child, let not sorrow crush thee! Lift up thy eyes to the approaching Saviour! He is the Master of Life. It is He who is always near on our long road of misery, but, alas, too often we do not see Him.

Neither does she see Him. Her eyes, bathed in tears, are fixed on the lifeless body of her only son. But Jesus sees her. Who, up to that time, had payed attention to a woman's tears? Who had shown pity with the misery of this slave, predestined to suffering? No one! O Jesus, Thou art the first!

"Whom when the Lord had seen, being moved with mercy towards her, He said to her: Weep not!"

No one as yet had said to woman: Weep not! Here, for the first time, she heard it and met with a consoler who accepts tears as prayers. Mother, weep no longer! His love

## The Widow of Naim.

and thy suffering rouse His compassion. But thou hast not yet seen Him, and if He came to meet thee and stood before thee, thou wouldst not know Him.

"And he came near and touched the bier. And they that carried him stood still."

The crowd, likewise, stood still. Silence everywhere. All are attentive; even sorrow is suspended.

"And he said: Young man, I say to thee, arise! And he that was dead sat up, and began to speak."

Great is the astonishment of all. Cries of joy and wonderment are heard on all sides. Whilst fear seizes the crowd, the mother is almost lost in her sudden happiness. But coming to, she stretches out her trembling arms to embrace the son, whose eyes sparkle again with life, and to tear away the winding sheets that bound him, and now the flexible arms of her son embrace her in return. Both fall down at the feet of Jesus to adore and glorify Him in token of their gratitude.

Holy Scripture is silent about all this; it expresses all in the simple sentence:

"And He gave him back to his mother. And there came a fear on them all: and they glorified God, saying: A great prophet is risen up among us, and God hath visited His people."

Where can we find a more striking image of the spiritual resurrection Jesus continues to operate in the souls of men? For, though by this miracle He intended to dry the tears of a mother, He wanted also to teach all men to seek in Him, for themselves and others dear to them, but dead to His love, the supernatural life, that the influx of divine grace alone can restore.

In a hidden way the Saviour is always near us, and tears shed before Him, He receives as prayers; and upon Him they exercise an influence quite different from what they do upon the hearts of our fellow men. Always remember that Jesus went to meet the widow in her sorrow; never forget, O woman, destined more than man to suffering, that it is for thee, who art mother, whose heart is more sensible, whose organism more delicate, He is waiting. Since His coming on earth, thou hast in Him, if thou wilt, an almighty consoler, a friend and confidant in all thy sad hours.

Poor women, poor mothers, what is there

you have not to suffer? Those you love are taken away from you by sickness, by war, by vice, by error! So many dangers for the body, so many for the soul! How numerous are they who are rapt up in the shrouds of incredulity or of a wicked life! How many are dead! With tears in your eyes, you admit the fact. They resist the cry of their conscience, your affectionate pleadings, even the warnings of Providence! All seems lost, and you unable to obtain the health of their body or the conversion of their soul! Take courage, then, and learn how to suffer. Tears shed before God have the power to resuscitate the dead. A day will come, a last hour, when a ray from the heart of Jesus shall shine upon you, when you shall understand, too, the reason of this long and cruel sickness, of this humiliating trial that nothing on earth could sooth . . . . . . A day will come on which this dead youth, your son,—those rapt up in the winding sheets of error, who may be your father, your brother, your husband, shall hear the divine voice. Jesus, then, will manifest Himself to them and to you. He will stretch out His hand or speak the word of authority: and your sick will recover, your beloved dead will listen again to the voice of reason and religion. They will pray with you, with you they shall go down on their knees before God . . . . you will have saved them.

# THE WOMEN WHO SERVE JESUS.

JESUS was sojourning at Capharnaum, a city on the laughing border of Lake Tiberias. His usual Sabbath task, instruction at the synagogue, being done, He with James and John who, of late, had attached themselves to Him, entered the house of Simon and Andrew.

Simon, whose birthplace was the neighboring Bethsaida, was married here. At his house Jesus considered Himself at home, since intercourse between Him and His disciples had become more and more familiar. To re-establish the wonderful familiarity of the paradisic days of innocence, was one of the objects of the Saviour's coming. From error and vice He wanted to call fallen humanity to the most intimate alliance with God. But who had fallen deeper than woman, so cruelly abused by egotism and the fierce passions of men?

Now "Simon's wife's mother lay in a fit of fever: and forthwith they tell Him of her. And coming to her he lifted her up, taking her by the hand: and immediately the fever left her, and she ministered unto them."

Sick and bedridden! Indeed, the picture of fallen humanity, and, especially, of the condition into which woman had fallen. Thus from the beginning of His public career, Jesus comes to her, and His disciples asked Him to heal her. Why? Is His own heart not bent upon it? However, the Saviour wants this prayer as a reparation of all the wrong man has done her. "And standing over her, he commanded the fever and it left her."

Standing at the side of the sick woman, Jesus recalls to men the respect due to her whom He has restored to her former dignity. And He commanded the fever. By Thy authority alone, O Lord, this poor patient recovers her health, and comes back to that double life of body and soul that had been almost suppressed in her. But it does not satisfy Thee and Thy loving designs to favor her with Thy presence, to stand at her side, to grant her Thy grace, to command the fever to leave her, no, that does not seem sufficient to Thee, dear Saviour: Thou art decided to restore her primitive nobility, the nobility of the days of innocence, and raise her even to a higher one.

"And taking the woman by the hand He lifted her up."

It must be the "Lord" and no one else; for who else could have thought of such a cure? Who else would have felt strength enough to face the custom of centuries, which, in its frightful and wide-spread corruption, even among the Jewish people, treated woman as the slave of man? In her own eyes as well as in those of men she can be raised only by the esteem with which the Saviour surrounds her. At this moment, at the side of the woman, He wants to bring about this double recovery; He wants to increase His favors to her who more and more excites His compassion, and, by this proof of predilection, give a remedy to her, the downtrodden and oppressed of the human race.

"Jesus takes her by the hand."

He lifts her to Himself. Woman, henceforth, shall understand His heart, whose secrets He will reveal unto her and whose burning flames she shall feel and see.*)

O woman, understand this elevation in the adoption that a God intimates to thee by the direct help He gives to raise thee up. By a common effort, by the union of His power and thy weakness, shall be brought about thy recovery.

The woman is not mistaken; intelligence is given her; she feels a new life pulse through her veins: "Immediately the fever left her." And rising up, "she ministered to them."

It was meal time. To show her gratitude as well as her perfect recovery, she, at once, prepared the viands, set them on the table, and presented them to Jesus and His companions.

The Evangelist notices here a hasty eagerness which is not reported of any other sick person cured by the Saviour.

\* \* \*

---

\*) Blessed Margaret Mary Alacocque.

## The Women Who Serve Jesus.

The Gospel also tells us of other women that served the Saviour on His journeys through Palestine.

The Jewish scribes and doctors, to be unhampered by material cares in their intercourse with their disciples, were usually accompanied by women. Jesus followed this custom.

"And it came to pass afterwards, that He traveled through the cities and towns preaching and evangelizing the kingdom of God; and the Twelve with Him. And certain women, who had been healed of evil spirits and infirmities: Mary who is called Magdalen, out of whom He had cast seven devils, and Joanna the wife of Chusa, Herod's steward, and many others who ministered to Him out of their substance."*)

Besides those named by the Evangelist we have to mention Mary, the Mother of Jesus; Salome, the mother of the Zebedees; Mary of Cleophas, mother of the three other Apostles, the sons of Alpheus and brothers of Jesus, and doubtless also His sisters of Nazareth,**) Esther and Thamar, of whom tradition tells us only the names.

---
*) Luke, VIII. 1—8.
**) It is well known that among the Jews cousins were called brothers and sisters.

"The Gospel shows us only women serving the Lord," says a learned theologian of the XII. century. "They had pledged all their property to assure His daily food, and had charged themselves with furnishing His necessaries. He Himself was the most humble servant of His disciples: He served them at table, washed their feet, and we have no proof that He ever received any service from them or, in fact, from any other man; women ministered to all the wants of His humanity."

At this stage of the Redemption, woman, roused from the sleep of slavery, becomes conscious of her dignity. Hardly rehabilitated herself, she becomes an apostle, sharing every effort in the work of Redemption and partaking of all that restores and elevates. And thus St. Paul writes of her:

"Have we no power to carry about a woman, a sister, as well as the rest of the Apostles, and the brethren of the Lord, and Cephas?" *)

O Virgin Mary, thou art there in the midst of these women, as the type of all Redemption and of all sanctity; thou art there, the perfect

---
*) I. Cor., IX. 5.

model of all those whom the Law of the Gospel forms for the service of Jesus.

Soon these holy women of Judea shall find followers and sisters wherever the Apostles shall preach the doctrine of the Saviour. Numerously they shall arise, both from among the Barbarians and the Greek and Roman world. And what a surprise to the whole world are these women consecrated to the daily service of the Saviour! They will renounce their riches and sacrifice their pride, they will quit the opulence of the palace and built sanctuaries for Thee, O Jesus, wherein to live at Thy feet. Others shall confess Thee before the executioner. O Christ, adored in all centuries, woman shall continue to serve Thee according to the wants and necessities of to-day's social condition in the same Apostolic spirit: her personality and social action are progressing and developing with them. And to serve Thee better, she is always daring more: in the poverty of the cloister she hides with poverty; in prisons, with vice, to bring thither purity and the grace of Redemption; in the hospitals, with suffering. But always with Thee, Lord, whose image she carries valiantly and triumphantly on her breast, to show that her heart beats but for Thee, in the weaknesses of human frailty and the persecutions of the world. What sacrifices she makes, what exquisite and celestial joys she finds in following Thee and pleasing Thee, will never be told.

And although the great multitude of Christian women cannot follow the three evangelical councils, their hearts beat no less for Thee and, likewise, live of Thy divine life. For neither place nor exployment constitute membership with Christ, but union with Him.

And to suffer, work, and pray in union with the Heart of Jesus, every day, is the Christian's sole and whole perfection.

## The Woman under an Issue of Blood.
## The Daughter of Jairus.

ONE morning, in the second year of His public life, Jesus approached the shores of Lake Genesareth. The crowd from which He had fled the evening before, recognized His barge and eagerly awaited His landing. One among them, in particular, the publican (revenue-collector) Levi, later an apostle, showed his joy over the return of the Master by inviting Him to a festival. Jesus with His disciples accepted the invitation and joined the guests at Levi's house. Meanwhile, the Pharisees and Scribes, who constantly kept themselves informed of the doings and whereabouts of the Saviour, had entered the open banquet hall, and, not daring to blame Jesus personally, addressed the Apostles, saying: "Why is it that your Master and you eat and drink with publicans and sinners?" *) The Apostles echoed their astonishment. Then Jesus answered in these admirable words: "They that are in health need not the physician, but they that are ill. Go then and learn what this meaneth: I will mercy and not sacrifice. For I am not come to call the just, but sinners." Then came to him the disciples of John, saying: "Why do we and the Pharisees fast often, but thy disciples do not fast?" And Jesus says to them: "Can the children of the bridegroom mourn as long as the bridegroom is with them? But the days will come, when the bridegroom shall be taken away from them, and then they shall fast." While He was speaking to them, a certain ruler from Capharnaum came up and addressed Him, saying: "Lord, my daughter is about dying, but come, lay thy hand upon her, and she shall live." And Jesus, rising up, followed him with His disciples.

During this, no doubt hasty, walk—for the

---
*) Matt. IX. 11—15.

father was in a hurry to get back to his dying child—Jesus, turning suddenly to the crowd, said:

"Who hath touched my garments?" *) As all protested their innocence: "Master," said Peter, "thou seest the multitude thronging thee, and sayest thou who hath touched me?"

"And Jesus said: Somebody hath touched me; for I know that virtue is gone out of from me."

Now a woman, who had suffered from an issue of blood for twelve years and spent her substance on all kinds of physicians, without receiving any help from them, had said within herself: "If I but touch the hem of His garment, I shall be healed." She had done so and had felt the virtue of the Saviour. Ashamed and trembling she approaches and, falling down at His feet, confesses her suffering and what she had done for relief. Jesus demanded this humble confession of her sickness, that constituted a legal impurity. He desired it rather as an act of humility than as a confession of His omnipotence. This woman had suffered much, and worldly science had pronounced her incurable. With what con-

---
*) Mark, V. 25—43.

fidence and hope do not we, too, approach the physician who can cure soul and body, when, under similar circumstances, we are persuaded that human help is of no avail.

Woman, thou hast done well by coming to Jesus to touch respectfully His garment, believing that at that very moment He will relieve thee. Yes, instantly His virtue is felt by thee, thou art healed. Yet thou alone didst feel that virtue, not the multitude thronging and pushing from all sides, as Peter observed, but who had come without any heartfelt wants, without any ardent prayers, simply from curiosity or, perhaps, with evil design. Only dispositions of the soul, a living faith and deep humility, render our connection with God fruitful; without them the most favorable circumstances remain fruitless.

When Jesus saw the poor woman humbling herself still more at His feet and thanking Him for His goodness, He addressed these life-giving words to her:

"Daughter, thy faith hath made thee whole, go in peace."

"Daughter"! Such is the new title that Jesus gives to fallen and suffering womankind.

It is the title of adoption. He gives it also to the sick woman whose divine consoler He had just been. "Daughter", this single word of love reveals to her, aye, to the whole human family, hitherto still trembling before its false deities, the new familiar intercourse which the God-Man came to establish between Heaven and earth. Woman, especially, stood in need of hearing, first of all, these adorable words of the Law of Grace. Poor woman, arise in confidence; open thy heart to the love of Him Who alone has the word that heals. Arise! Understand and comprehend thy new dignity. He calls thee daughter, and His word effects what it says: rejoice in thy recovery from bodily infirmity, but much more in thy new dignity—of being a child of God.

"As he was yet speaking, there cometh one to the ruler of the synagogue, saying to him: Thy daughter is dead, trouble him not. And Jesus hearing these words, answered the father of the maid: Fear not! Believe only, and she shall be safe." Constantly the Saviour forbids fear and exhorts to a living faith. And this necessary faith Jesus is willing to give to all who demand it, and, frequently, a single word of His makes it plain: — "Only believe, and she shall be safe."

The faith of the woman under an issue of blood had quite a different life and energy. She faces all obstacles and concentrates all her efforts on reaching Jesus. And whilst she, by and for her faith, obtained instantaneous relief and received the consoling name of daughter, the young maid is lying on her couch, dying—dead,—an image of humanity plunged into vice and error; an image also of her sex, helplessly immersed in spiritual sloth. Hence the girl needed another to intercede for her, and Christ heard the prayer of her father.

When Jesus came to the house, friends and neighbors had gathered there, and the body was about to be embalmed. The mournful cries of the hired women mingled with the sad tunes of the flute players.

"And going in he saith to them: Why make ye this ado? The damsel is not dead but sleepeth. And they laughed him to scorn."

And for this mockery they were all put out. To witness the divine works is a singular favor, which those alone receive who have the proper disposition. The father and the mother of the dead girl had been prepared by their sorrow to believe in the almighty power of the Saviour, since by that very sorrow they had been driven to Him and had obtained the benefit of His presence. As He is now with them, their agony is suspended, their hearts beat with hope. Jesus, therefore, together with His three favorite disciples, admits them to the death chamber. Then, taking the girl by the hand, He raises His voice, that voice divine, unknown to her, and commands her, saying: "Damsel, I say to thee, arise!"

Who but God can command the dead? "And immediately the damsel arose and walked." Astounded and over-happy, even the parents forgot what care the condition of the child required. Not so Jesus, who called them to their duty, saying: "Give her to eat," and thereby showed a solicitude more attentive and more tender than maternal love itself. "So fatherly as Thou, O Lord, none; so tender as Thou, none!"*)

Blessed therefore, are those children whose parents go for them to Jesus, asking Him to lead them by His hand.

---

*) "Tam pater nemo, tam bonus nemo." Tertull.

Happy also all those who steadily fix their eyes upon the end of life, and in the light of death dispose all their actions.

But why are we told these two wonderful and successive facts, one concerning an aged woman, the other, a girl of twelve, each unable any longer to profit of human affection, intelligence or science? To convince us more and more of the absolute need we have of God, all along the path of life, and that outside of the manifest order, divinely established for the guidance of man, our whole being, soul and body, languishes, suffers, and dies when separated from the source of light. Woman, especially, as guardian of the hearth, falls deeper, the farther she recedes from the grace of Redemption, as from Christ Himself she has received the mission to communicate to the family, and through the family to society, that regenerating fire, that totality of Christian life, which alone will answer our innermost aspirations and longings after the ideal and real happiness.

Oh woman, He Who healed thee from thy infirmity; damsel, He Who took thee by the hand, restoring thee to life, — also wants to be your guide and support for the remainder of your earthly pilgrimage. Do not withdraw your confidence from Him. Listen attentively and obediently to His words. He tells you, the greatest obstacle to the development of the spiritual life He has just communicated to you, is selfishness, narrow selfishness, that strangles mind and heart by concentrating them upon our own little self. If you want to vanquish that subtle enemy, who is all the more destructive the less he is perceived, go out of your own selves, aim at doing God's work, and by Him and with Him advance whatever is morally good and beautiful.

And thou, young maiden of our days, resuscitated by the word of Jesus, march on in life on the wings of youth, but be on thy guard against false doctors, who wish to take thee by the hand. They, like the flute players in the house of Jairus, have heard and still hear the words of the Master; but they answer with a sneer. They want thee to be an unbeliever and a free-thinker, alike to them. Be on thy guard against their soft but lying words, against the chains that await thee at the first denial of thy Saviour. Cling to Him

## 74 *The Woman under an Issue of Blood.*

and His infinite goodness! Inflame thy heart with love for Jesus! His word exhorts thee to perfection: excelsior, rise higher, excelsior, aim highest. God is that aim. With the clear eye of wisdom select the road that leads thee to Him.*)

---

*) Thus a certain noble young lady understood life, when, at the age of twenty, she wrote:

"Death does not surprise, but finds ready, those who, without trouble or sadness, have kept before their mind the thought of it as an ever burning light for their guidance on the paths here below."

And again: "My God, open for me those pure and luminous spaces, far beyond this earth; let my soul, in its mighty and sure flight, touch Heaven with its wings, to show Thee my impatience and the sole aim of its exertions."

(Gabrielle Thépault de Breignou. Died May 11. 1889.)

# MARY MAGDALEN.

### THE LAW OF PARDON MADE KNOWN TO FALLEN WOMAN.

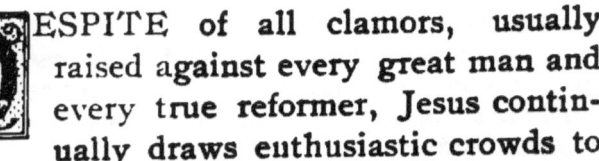ESPITE of all clamors, usually raised against every great man and every true reformer, Jesus continually draws enthusiastic crowds to Himself. He is the friend of the people, who, in return, lovingly surround Him. Even the great and the rich think it an honor to receive Him.

Approachable by all, Jesus gives Himself to all classes of men and to all religious parties, in order to gain all for the truth. Good connections render the exchange of ideas easy, and enable one to influence the minds of others. We have to converse with, and live among, the men whom we want to lead. Diverging ideas do not necessarily exclude pleasant intercourse, nor a certain indulgence for men in good faith, nor compassion. According to the words of the Apostle, for a Christian "There is neither Greek nor Roman, neither slave nor freeman."

Such, however, was not the rule among the ruling sects in Israel. Men of narrow and violent dispositions, they invented one calumny after another to ruin the divine Saviour. But He paid no attention to them; He had not come to please men, but to lead sinners to His father. And thus we find Him at table with publicans and sinners, but also with His opponents, the Pharisees. From the table of a Pharisee Jesus shall instruct us this time.

The host's name was Simon. He lived at Magdala, on the borders of Lake Tiberias, where he was considered a person of great influence. In this town lived also a sinful woman, by the name of Mary, who, hereafter, shall become renowned not only in the pages of the Gospel, but also in the early history of Christianity, and, in fact, throughout the world until the end of time.

Mary was the sister of Martha and Lazarus. From rabbinic sources we learn that her parents died when she was quite young. Raised according to her rank, she acquired the knowledge of the Sacred Books. With her gifts of mind she united the charms of great beauty. From her place of birth, Magdala, she is called Mary of Magdala or, more commonly, Mary Magdalen. This title added to her name indicated to the Jews her high station. The house in which she was born was still shown in the first centuries of the Christian era. Magdala itself was a charming town, washed on its eastern side by the azure waves of the lake, and on the other sides surrounded by fertile plains covered with fruits and flowers. The Romans had stationed within its walls a garrison, that did not improve the bad odor in which the manners of its inhabitants stood. The misconduct of Mary can easily be explained from the nature of her surroundings.

Contemporary writers state she was married to a Doctor of the Law, named Paphus, who separated from her on account of her disorderly life.

By the Talmud and the Fathers of the early

Church, Pandera is named several times as her accomplice. Pandera was an officer in the Roman army at Magdala, groomsman of Paphus, charged to preside at the nuptial banquet and to conduct the bride solemnly to her new residence.

How was Mary drawn to Jesus? At what place, and under what circumstances, had she the happiness of seeing Him for the first time? That meeting probably took place at Naim, a town in the neighborhood of Magdala, the memorable day, on which the widow's son was raised from among the dead, which preceded the banquet at the house of Simon. There, lost in the multitude, but seen by the Seer of Israel, she, no doubt, received, by glance from His eyes, the light that manifested to her the slavery and shame of her life.

Now Jesus is approaching the city in which she lived. Hasten, Mary, hasten! Dost thou not know that He expects thee that very hour? Apparently she does; admiration and remorse push her towards Him, the giver of a new life.

"Shortly after the resurrection of the widow's son at Naim," says the commentator Simon of Cassia, "there was a banquet at Simon's, at which Jesus assisted; and Mary, still under the emotion of the miracle, went there to find Jesus." — "And behold a woman that was in the city, a sinner, when she knew that He sat at meat in the Pharisee's house, brought an alabaster box of ointment; and standing behind him at his feet; she began to wash his feet with her tears and wiped them with the hair of her head and kissed his feet, and anointed them with ointment."*)

General stupefaction took hold of the asssembly. Her proceeding seemed folly to all, one excepted.

Behold, then, that proud beauty with an unsavory name, behold her prostrate in repentance! She recognizes her Redeemer and, henceforth, she is determined to be no longer the slave of those who put shame where God wants love.

Contrary to custom, Mary of Magdala has loosed her long hair. Except when mourning, it was a shame to wear the hair unbound. Mary does not hesitate to thus testify to the depth of her sorrow and to the honor of Him who is to cleanse her. She brought with

---

*) Luke VII. 37 seq.

her a costly alabaster box with precious perfumes, to express her love and esteem for the Saviour. On solemn occasions the ancients made use of perfumes to anoint the guest of honor. At nuptial feasts this service was rendered the presiding Rabbi after he had tied the nuptial knot. All peoples of antiquity made use of perfumes at their festivities, but up to that time, the most extravagant had never poured out spikenard over the feet of a guest. According to contemporary historians, it was a royal offering.

How well is Mary inspired.

That bottle of perfumes was one of the presents she had received on her marriage morning to perfume herself with; and as it reminded her of her infidelity to the marriage vow, she now breaks it to indicate her break with, and separation from, the world. She pours it over the feet of the Saviour, that meek and compassionate judge, who is appeased by repentance, but unfortunately too often misunderstood by the world.

In her hands this ointment shall also become the symbol of her alliance with the Saviour, who alone shall possess her hereafter.

Tears, protestations, flames of love, rise,

rise up toward the heart of Jesus with these sweet-smelling clouds! Jesus, without the least effort to withdraw Himself, accepts the homage of the sinful woman.

The whole scene is an occasion for surprise, if not for indignation, to the host of the Saviour, the Pharisee Simon. At his place, in the midst of a banquet, in the presence of the most distinguished personages, a public woman addresses the Master in such a manner, and He, far from repelling her, allows her at His feet! "Indeed, if this man were a prophet," said the Pharisee within himself, "He would know surely who and what manner of woman this is that touches Him, that she is a sinner."

Simon is mistaken. He judges from appearances. One cannot be just without knowing the moving cause and the secret thoughts. Good people respect the liberty of others, they comment favorably on, or excuse, the apparently bad actions of others, they rather ignore evil, and feel compassion with the agonies of remorse and the tears of repentance. They share the joy of Heaven over one sinner who does penance and give thanks with him and for him.

Is Simon better than Mary? Was he just towards her when she lay on her knees before Jesus, Who repeatedly had proved His mission to him? No. He personifies that mediocrity, "which, unable to explain anything to itself by its own narrow views and intentions, does not understand the language that is spoken, and freely admits evil designs and base suspicions." (J. de Maistre.) Of a narrow, haughty, and inconsistent mind, he knows, neither to render homage to truth, nor can he understand — to bewail them generously —the weaknesses of the human heart in the errings of Mary; he condemns both the repenting sinner and the God Who pardons.

Then Jesus said to Simon: "Simon, I have somewhat to say to thee;" but he said: "Master, say it."

The Saviour, knowing the thoughts and sentiments of his host, wants to enlighten him and teach him the law of grace and pardon which He is about to introduce into the world. But as what He had to say for his instruction was somewhat humiliating, the divine Master first asks his permission. As the guest of Simon He has due regard for His host: He does not reveal his secret thoughts — that would humiliate him — He knows but too well that every word, to be acceptable and efficacious, must be meek and uttered at the proper moment. He also knows that truth does not germinate, grow, and bear fruit, if the soil is not prepared. Hence, in a cordial manner and in the simple conversational tone, Jesus said to Simon:

"A creditor had two debtors, the one owed him five hundred pence and the other fifty. And whereas they had not wherewith to pay, he forgave them both. Which therefore of the two loveth him most?"

What a change of scene! A moment ago Mary had entered, all eyes were fixed on her, a sneer or contemptible smile is on the faces of all present. She throws herself at the feet of Jesus; He seems not to notice it, He does not look, He lets her proceed…. But now all eyes are directed to Simon, who already suspicions that from a secret plaintif he shall be made a public defendant. Yet he must answer, though condemning himself when he says:

"I suppose that he whom he forgave most."

The Pharisee has judged between himself and the woman.

Jesus thereupon turns to Mary: by look

and word He places the former sinner before the zealot of the Law; and He condemns the zealot.

Recalling the custom of the Orient, which Simon had slighted, He said to him:

"Dost thou see this woman? I entered thy house, thou gavest me no water for my feet, but she with tears has washed my feet, and with her hair hath wiped them. Thou gavest me no kiss, but she, since she came in, hath not ceased to kiss my feet. My head with oil thou didst not anoint, but she with ointment hath anointed my feet. Wherefore I say to thee: Many sins are forgiven her, because she hath loved much. But to whom less is forgiven, he loveth less."

Behold now the Law of Pardon promulgated in the world, and first of all applied to woman, who had also been the first to sin! It behooved her, too, before all others to fall down at the feet of the Saviour, to ask, not recovery from bodily ailings, as multitudes do daily, but her moral rehabilitation for all the time to come.

Together with this Law of Pardon Jesus proclaims the Law of Justice, that forbids us to judge rashly and commands us to look into our own hearts before we blame others.

In this case the more so as the faults objected to are the very ones on which men are inexorable, but which they mostly provoke. And in regard to these faults, the Redeemer pronounces Himself in the most explicit and touching manner: the great public sinner for the first time is absolved by Him in the most solemn way:

"Many sins are forgiven her, because she hath loved much. But to whom less is forgiven, he loveth less."

Oh, may all be forgiven in Mary of Magdala, the personification of guilty humanity! Love of God is the reparation of all her faults; it remedies evil in its cause and effects. Love of God, too, makes us lead a holy life, but love of self with contempt of God leads to violation of the Law. Disorderly self-love caused the fall and ruin of Mary Magdalen; love of God produced in her repentance, that leads to self-denial and a life of purity and virtue.

"Placing His love at the head of the commandments," writes St. Paulinus of Nola, "God made it possible for all of us, insolvent as we are, to pay our debts. Let, therefore, no one say: I have nothing, I cannot pay.

Has not each one a heart? No sacrifices are asked of us, no costly offerings, no hard works: within ourselves we find wherewith to pay; for if anything is ours, it is our love. Give it to the Lord, and He is satisfied. And more than that, for, from a creditor, He wants to become our debtor."*)

As a cold zealot of the Law and an excessive observer of the Law's formalities, Simon can neither love his God nor his neighbor, for, says Jesus to him: "I have entered thy house, thou gavest me no water for my feet." He might have added — and Simon would have had to acknowledge the truth of it: "The sinner has come in here, and thou didst despise her." For the Law of the love of God not only enjoins on us its punctual observance, but also commands us to love God with our whole heart and our neighbor as ourselves, the culprit not excepted; for he, too, is God's creature.

As to Mary, the now converted sinner, she loved with the love of repentance, that possesses the mysterious power to annihilate sin and renew the soul, by giving birth to a new creature. There is another kind of love, that

---

*) Mgr. Lagrange, "Life of St. Paulinus."

which preserves the just in justice; but at bottom, both are the same,—the union of the soul with its God.

"Then Jesus said to Mary: "Thy sins are forgiven thee."

He spoke as God, and the guests understood it well; for they began to say within themselves: "Who is this that forgiveth sins also?" The Pharisees not only refused to recognize the divinity of the Saviour, but also felt displeased, that sin received such a prompt, large, and tender pardon. They shall never forgive that way, nor shall they ever teach the people that God forgives so readily. The conduct of Jesus condemns them—they grumble.

O Holy Church, thou alone dost absolve in truth; thou alone art the repose of the poor sinner! Who before thee spoke a re-assuring word? Not the doctors in Israel, not the prophets, not the priests, not the philosophers, not Plato nor the oracles . . . . but Jesus did forgive, and thou, in His name, canst do likewise, because He commands thee to do so.

After this manifestation of His divine meekness Jesus leaves the Pharisees. Their hardened hearts deserve no further instruction.

His last word is addressed to Mary of Magdala: "Thy faith hath made thee safe. Go in peace!"

To fully believe in some one, means to give him our esteem, our confidence, and affection. The more firmly we believe, the more these sentiments will develop within us. The grace of graces for a Christian is the happiness of being firmly rooted in the faith brought to this earth by Jesus. In it and by it we find light and joy of mind, widening and peace of heart. From this summit, the Christian can embrace the wonder world of grace and nature; there he can enjoy them in their fulness and be satiated with them. "For the glory of God hath enlightend them, and the Lamb is the lamp thereof."*)

"Peace be with you," was the customary salutation among the Jews, the sign by which they recognized each other, the wish they had for one another when they met. "Go in peace!" said the Saviour to her whom he had absolved. From Him these words are no longer a wish, they are a gift. "Go in peace!" Such is the sublime blessing of His heart and His parting word at this famous banquet.

---
*) Apoc. XXI. 28.

# THE ADULTEROUS WOMAN ABSOLVED BY JESUS.

THE feast of the Tabernacles, instituted by Moses in the memory of the forty years passed by the Jews under tents in the desert, is to be celebrated again with all its poetical solemnity in the City of Jerusalem. During the eight days of its celebration the Hebrews dwell in tents, made of foliage, and chant the grand Alleluja of thanksgiving; lambs and kids are sacrificed; priests pour water and wine on the altar of the Lord; and the people, singing psalms, march around the altar with branches of palm and myrtle. The greater solemnity of the eighth day draws also a greater crowd to the Temple; for it is the last day, "good and joyous, the great Hosanna."

Will Jesus go to the Temple? So the pilgrims ask one another. The new prophet is the talk of the people. He excites their curiosity and inspires them with admiration or hatred.

"The Jews therefore sought him on the festival day, and said: Where is he? And there was much murmuring among the multitude concerning him. For some said: He is a good man. And others said: No, but he seduceth the people. Yet no man spoke openly of him for fear of the Jews."*)

His enemies, so often dumfounded by Him, plotted anew how to undermine His influence. This "impostor" has seduced the people long enough, they said, He has become a menace to the nation. Thus the bitter fight was kept up even on festival days.

Jesus is the object of their conversation; all speak of Him according to their good or evil will; all expect Him; they were not deceived.

Whilst He thus formed the object of discussion, He quit Nazareth forever, passing through Galilee and Samaria, through the vine-yards of Saron, between the Thabor and Lake Genesareth, and, crossing the Jordan

---
*) John, VII. 11—13.

## Absolved by Jesus.

twice, He ascended from Jericho to Jerusalem by the route of the Romans.

The doctors of the Law, together with the Scribes and Pharisees, had sent out soldiers to seize Him, but, having failed in this project, they hoped to catch Him by a snare.

Towards the middle of the festival season, Jesus went to the Temple, teaching there, and many believed in Him, even of those that were sent by His enemies to catch Him.

"And the Scribes and the Pharisees bring unto Him a woman taken in adultery, and they set her in the midst. And said to Him: Master, this woman was even now taken in adultery. Now Moses in the Law commandeth us to stone such a one. But what sayest Thou? And this they said tempting Him that they might accuse Him."*)

"It was in the midst of those noisy festivities, called by Plutarch the bacchanalia of the Jews, among a crowd of strangers from everywhere, that this woman had shamefully forgotten herself in the universal run after sinful and worldly pleasures."**)

"Death was the sentence passed by all earthly lawgivers upon the culprit. Whipped

---
*) John, VIII. 8—11.
**) Life of Our Lord. By the Abbé Camus, page 27.

from her conjugal home, chased by the populace through the streets of the town, exposed on an elevated stone in the public place, then placed on an ass and lead through the city, she heard nought but condemnation and cries for her blood for a sin that the law hardly forbade her husband.\*)

In difficult cases the Jews usually consulted a distinguished rabbi. In accordance with this custom, but principally from malice, the Pharisees addressed Jesus. The culprit, in the opinion of the experts of the Law, was to be hanged, burned, or stoned according as she was the wife of a Jew, or a priest, or only betrothed. It appears that this woman was only betrothed.

This serious and stirring fact interrupted the teaching of Jesus. If He condemns the culprit, He is not the meek prophet of the New Law He was teaching and will lose His prestige; if He absolves her, He despises the Mosaic prescriptions and opposes them. How can He escape the dilemma? His enemies already rejoice.

It is morning. The rays of the rising sun are reflected brilliantly on the gilt coping of

---

\*) Legouvé, "*Histoire morale des femmes.*".

the Temple, although penetrating less intensely the place where Jesus was teaching. Their mild light brought out wonderfully the intelligent and kind features of the Saviour.

The culprit before Him is wrapt up in the long veil of the Jewess, as she morally was in shame and despair. Near her stand the accusers clamoring for her condemnation. The crowd is silent, waiting for a word; but Jesus also keeps silent; bowing Himself down, He wrote with His finger on the ground.

Thus the rabbis acted when they wished to evade an answer. "When, therefore, they continued asking Him, He lifted Himself up, and said to them: He that is without sin among you, let him first cast a stone upon her. And again stooping down, He wrote on the ground."

What did Jesus write? Did He write a sentence, or the faults of her accusers? Some interpreters are of that opinion, but no one knows anything certain. What is certain, though, is that "they, hearing this, went out one by one, beginning at the eldest. And Jesus alone remained, and the woman standing in the midst."

What! Not one of her accusers, these

zealots of the Law, has the courage to attest his virtue and to apply the Law by taking up the revenging stone? Their guilty conscience forbids it. They sneak away dumb and confounded.

Thou alone, kindest of Masters, hast the power of placing the mighty face to face with their iniquities, to make them feel their own shame, and recognize themselves more guilty than the weak woman they prosecute with Pharisaic justice!

History, indeed, tells us that depravity was then at its height in the Synagogue, even among those that outwardly professed the most scrupulous observance of the legal prescriptions. The word and example of Jesus were repulsed, if not despised by them. The evil was such that no remedy could stop it. Yet a little while and an order from Heaven will be executed by the Roman legions, and that godforsaken nation shall be made a warning forever to all impious people.

The woman now being left to herself, Jesus said to her: "Woman, where are those that accused thee? Hath no man condemned thee?"

During this whole scene, the tenderness of

the Saviour is manifested even in His attitude. As long as the culprit is surrounded by her accusers and a crowd of curious people, He does not ask her a single question, He does not look at her, He even diverts the attention of the public from her. He thereby wishes to teach us how carefully Christian compassion must treat the humiliating faults of others. Moreover, He alone is without sin; He alone, therefore, according to the judgment rendered, is entitled to throw the first stone at her; yet He alone protects and He alone defends her . . . . . He, the eternal brightness and sanctity, facing this despised and dishonored woman, keeps silent. And if His ire is roused, it is against the more guilty who, lying to their conscience, accuse others, whilst they themselves are sinners.

"The example of Jesus Christ proves to us," says a contemporary writer, showing the injustice of our customs and our laws, "that, when we are in presence of two culprits guilty of the same crime, of whom one is set free and the other condemned, the indignation against the impunity of the one involuntarily provokes in us a sentiment of pity for the other. Thus in the name of the most just rigor that should attain the woman, do not absolve him who, as an excuse for his wrong, sets forward nothing but his own vicious inclination. The absolute, everlasting, and theoretic amnesty of adultery committed by men is one of the greatest scandals of justice."

Lord, the crowd of accusers, the Pharisees and hypocrites, have vanished from Thy presence as nightbirds before the light!

Now alone with the woman, Jesus speaks to her. Those in the highest stations, those morally and socially superior, should always stoop down to the little ones or the guilty ones, to lead them away from sin and to prepare them for a true repentance, that alone deserves pardon.

To save men, Providence wonderfully disposes things to bring about such happy encounters. Frequently the sinner finds everything prosperous around him; he has no thought of repentance; by estranging his friends, by their contempt and cruelty towards him, Jesus leads him to His feet. And it thus happens that when the world prosecutes a fault, the sinner finds an equitable judge and forgiveness.

•

"Hath no man condemned thee?"

"No man, Lord."

By these simple words, Thou, O Lord, wishest to gain this woman, to make her understand still better that to Thee alone she owes her deliverance, and that, after her example, the guilty women of all centuries, buried in shame and trampled under foot by men, have but to return to Thee, O God, Whose heart is open to them whenever they call on Thee. When Thou approachest, where will be the accusers?

Fear no longer, poor, contrite and humbled culprit! Lift up thy eyes to thy Redeemer, and from the source of thy tears, smile at the mercy of Jesus! He alone knows the facts and their excuses, the regrets and the secret good resolutions. He alone is merciful in His justice. Listen, then, to the sentence of the Master and meditate upon it with all the powers of gratitude and love!

"Neither will I condemn thee!"

Jesus has changed thy heart; thou art absolved before Heaven and earth, before the angels and all men of good will. Reading with attention in the pages of the Gospel and observing what takes place around us, we have to confess: indeed, the judgments of earth are more severe than the judgments of Heaven. David recognized it when he said: "I am in great straits, but it is better that I should fall in the hands of the Lord (for His mercies are many) than into the hands of men."*)

O blessed Christ, Thou showest Thy tender mercy above all to fallen and despised woman, and to her Thou sayest: "Neither will I condemn thee." Thus in a special manner Thou declarest Thyself to be her Saviour. She is before Thee, dumb and silenced by her accusers and judges. Frequently accused, she was always condemned without ever finding an advocate. All the burden of human faults fell upon her. And in spite of the vaunted XIXth century progress that same injustice is still upheld in the courts of some civilized countries. (cf. Code Napoleon.)

Poor, repenting, sinful woman, have recourse to God, seek his priest! He knows the frailty of human nature and sees no difference in thy downfall and that of another. Judging thee alone and in the pre-

---
*) II. Kings, XXIV. 14.

## Absolved by Jesus.

sence of God, he will say to thee: I absolve thee, I will not condemn thee. Go in peace!

The right of pardoning, the sole privilege of God, has become in the Church and Christian society the most beautiful privilege of authority. The Church has multiplied pardons after the example of her Founder and penetrated her heart with His meekness. And in Christian society, sentiments of compassion, pity, and forgiveness, formerly unknown, surround the guilty.*)

But to His absolution the Saviour added an admonition. "Go," He said to her, "and now sin no more!"

---

\*) "The quality of mercy is not strain'd ;
  It droppeth as the gentle rain from Heaven
  Upon the place beneath ; it is twice bless'd ;
  It blesseth him that gives, and him that takes :
  It is mightiest in the mightiest ; it becomes
  The throned monarch better than his crown ;
  His sceptre shows the force of temporal power,
  The attribute to awe and majesty,
  Wherein doth sit the dread and fear of kings :
  But mercy is above his sceptred sway,
  It is enthroned in the hearts of kings,
  It is an attribute of God Himself ;
  And earthly power doth then show likest God's
  When mercy seasons justice."
    Shakespeare, Merchant of Venice, Act. IV.

Go, return home to thy work, to thy daily duties; nothing else I ask of thee; nor do I impose on thee any legal or special penalty: —but sin no more! Then, when no longer a sinner, the esteem of Redemption's grace and price shall steadily grow in thee and become in thy soul a canticle of praise and love.

Restored by Jesus to the supernatural life, this pardoned sinner understands how the Almighty takes pleasure in transforming impure, stagnant waters into limpid and refreshing dews, and in making of the sinner an apostle for so many of her sisters, who, as she, are waiting for the hand that uplifts and pardons.

Who, indeed, knows better how to remedy evil in others than she who has suffered herself? Who is more deft in lifting the fallen than the one who has fallen herself?

# JUSTA, THE CANANEAN.

**FOR HER FAITH JESUS GRANTS HER PETITION.**

ALREADY in the first year of His public teaching, Jesus found many enemies among the Pharisees in Judea. Therefore, He left that country and, with His disciples, traversed the valleys and mountains of Galilee and then directed His steps towards the confines of Syria and Phenicia, where the remembrance of Elias and his stay at the widow's in Sarepta was still alive in the memory of many.

Syria, like Judea, was for the Jews a sacred country, because it paid the tithes and celebrated the Sabbath Year. Hence Jews were allowed to travel there at any time without incurring legal impurity.

The fame of Jesus had already gone beyond the limits of Palestine. According to St. Matthew, it had spread over all Syria, Idumea, and the neighboring countries. Travelers spoke of the novelty of His doctrine and extolled His innumerable miracles. On this journey, Jesus approached a city, probably Tyre, when a woman of Canaan, who came out of these coasts, crying out, said to Him: "Have mercy on me, O Lord, Thou son of David: my daughter is grievously troubled by a devil."*)

Cananean, according to St. Matthew, because of her origin; Syro-Phenician, according to St. Luke, who had in view the place where she lived, she is called Justa in a work of the fourth century.**)

Compassion and suffering drive this woman to the feet of Jesus. No one can help her; all human assistance has been in vain. He alone can deliver her child from the evil that torments her. It is no ordinary sickness; Justa knows it and she is not afraid to say so. But

---

*) Matt., XV. 21—28.
**) The Clementines. — Her daughter the same author calls Berenice.

whence did this woman draw the faith that the Jews, constant observers of the Saviour's miracles, so obstinately refused Him?

God has secret adorers and friends among all men of good will, who seek Him with an upright heart and live up to the dictates of their conscience, although, at times, erroneous. Word of God, Thou speakest secretly to the soul that, though ignorant of religious truth, loves sincerity. Thou stirrest it by Thy grace and sometimes renderest it capable of actions and sentiments even superior to those of many of Thy faithful. How much more dost thou do so, when, blended with their good desires, Thou seest suppliant tears and hearest the cry: "Have pity on me!"

Jesus apparently paid no attention to the woman; He and His disciples continued their march on this much frequented and dusty road under a parching sun. The woman, behind them, keeps up her cries and her tears—a picture of human sorrow and misery that manifested itself in the midst of silent, passible nature.

Will Jesus not listen to her? Will He remain insensible to the supplications of her sorrow? Shall it be in vain that Justa repeats in His ears these heartrending wails of which a mother alone has the secret!

"And His disciples came and besought Him, saying: Send her away (grant her prayer), for she crieth after us." They spoke thus, because, ordinarily, they did not appeal without obtaining His favors.

To their surprise, Jesus does not grant their petition, saying: "I was not sent but to the lost sheep of the house of Israel."

They are near the city; the sight of strangers and, still more, the cries of the woman, attract attention. Why did this woman follow the new-comers? . . . . Trying to escape from her and from the indiscreet looks of curiosity, Jesus enters a house. What shall the poor woman do now? To see Him, to make Him hear her prayers, had been her hope; but now even this chance is gone. Must she return home to behold again the sad spectacle of her tormented daughter? Never! With manly courage she enters the house and, throwing herself at the feet of Jesus, she says: "Lord, help me."

Unlike the Jews, she does not ask Him to come to her house to heal her daughter, but that He will it only, and her beloved child shall be safe — a single act of His will is sufficient.

"It is not good," said Jesus to her, "to take the bread from the children, and to cast it to the dogs."*)

A surprisingly harsh word from the Saviour! Yet He told His disciples before: let the children of the favored nation have their fill first. They, in virtue of the divine promise, have the first right to the favors and graces of the Messiah.

The Cananean, however, is not hurt, nor does she lose her confidence in Jesus; she does not leave Him, murmuring and indignant, as many others would have done. Though of the Cananean race, hated and despised by the Jews, she has the faith of the children of God. Oh, inestimable power of an humble faith, that, at all events and under all circumstances, even when Heaven seems to be against us, leaves unshaken our sentiments and convictions, our will and attitude towards God!

"But she said: Yea, Lord! for the whelps

---

*) As in our days the Mohamedans call the Christians "giaurs", so in those days the Jews called the heathens "dogs" and despised them as impure.

also eat of the crumbs that fall from the table of their masters."

Accepting the comparison, she makes a weapon out of it against the refusal of Jesus: —Well, suppose I am one of these dogs, are they refused the crumbs that fall from the table? Woman, thy retort is sublime; can Jesus continue His refusal? Has His tender and compassionate heart not suffered enough from this long resistence? God often takes pleasure in being vanquished by us.

"Woman, thy faith is great, be it done to thee as thou wilt."

What! This infidel and despised woman, this dog, as she was called, is granted such a power by Jesus that He submits His will to hers? "Be it done to thee as thou wilt." Henceforth salvation comes from faith, but not, as the Jews believed, from being born a child of Abraham.—Her unflinching faith overcomes the divine will formally expressed and even modifies, as it were, the plan of evangelization. What wilt Thou, O Lord, refuse to the prayers of the just, and where are Thy unalterable decrees? What is there that Thy dearest friend cannot obtain? What wilt Thou refuse to those whose will is Thy will, whose hearts, at Thy feet, breathe the purest love, whose very aspirations and continuous self-immolations have but one object in view: the salvation of souls, the grandeur of Thy kingdom, and the manifestation of Thy glory?

Christian mothers, ask of God whatever you will, especially in the supernatural order; do not be discouraged by a first refusal! After the example of this admirable woman, persevere in spite of all obstacles, even when desperation seems to stare you in the face. Perhaps the minutes or hours the Cananean spent in supplication represent for you as many months or years of prayer, of suffering, of tears!

Everywhere one hears the distressing complaint: I have prayed in vain! Did we really pray? Did we pour out our soul before God with that sublime energy of faith and love that is capable of transporting mountains? Again, did we give Almighty God the proper time in which He will be pleased to hear our prayers?

As a rule, He does not, as He did here, perform miracles, brilliant and instantaneous. He works out His designs slowly, by degrees, under cover, as it were.

The prayers of Monica did not obtain the

sudden conversion of Augustine, but first a break with his former associates, then a trip to Rome, next the meeting with St. Ambrose, and finally his conversion, after twenty years of maternal suffering.

Let us, therefore, have recourse to prayer! And behold what God will do: little by little He will remove obnoxious influences and bring about favorable surroundings; He will, perhaps, change the material conditions of life; He will punish; if necessary, send sickness or death itself to change the soul hitherto under the dominion of the Devil, and grant it a final repentance. The world is full of this kind of wonders, — wonders of divine love, brought about in silence of long duration, under cover of the natural laws.

The day will come when we, too, shall clearly see that a multitude of facts, apparently natural, i. e., the product of material forces and free will, were due exclusively to special arrangements of divine Providence, provoked by Christian faith and persevering prayer.

As to the daughter of the Cananean woman, she was healed that very hour. Next to the sorrow of the mother, nothing could move the heart of Jesus so much as the pitiable condition of the daughter, possessed by the Devil and tortured by him in soul and body. "Be it done to thee as thou wilt," were the words of Jesus, and the demon left her at once. Arriving home, the mother found her delivered from her torturer — natural, calm, and free.

Happy return! By the grace of Jesus the ties between mother and daughter become stronger and closer. They had asked for bodily health only, but they received the redeeming grace of eternal salvation at the same time. What Providence aims at in sending sorrows and misery, is the salvation of souls; such is the end God has in view, the only one worthy of His sovereign goodness. And, really, these two were among the first Christian women that, by their influence and wealth, helped in the establishment of the new-born Church. So say the revelations of Catharine Emmerich, and add: "Justa resolved never more to visit a heathen temple, but to strictly follow the teachings of Jesus."

Son of God, for men of good will, for upright and sincere souls, Thy words are consoling and quickening in this vale of tears; they also lead to life everlasting!

# MARTHA AND MARY.

#### WOMAN RECEIVES JESUS AT HER HOME.

IT is at the house of Martha, near Jerusalem, on the incline of a hill, studded with trees and laid out in garden beds, that Jesus deigns to stay for a day.

Martha, tradition tells us, was born at Bethany, a year or two after the birth of the Saviour. From rabbinic sources we learn, moreover, that her mother, Euchary, was a descendant of the ancient kings of Israel. Her father, Theophilus, of Syrian extraction, was governor of the larger part of the Palestine coast and possessed extensive landed estates at Magdala, Bethany, and Jerusalem.

Both parents had become disciples of Jesus, but died already in the earlier part of the Saviour's public life; hence we hear only of their children in the Gospel.

Martha had a brother, called Lazarus, renowned for his talents and highly esteemed for his virtues, and a younger sister, named Mary, who was born at Magdala. This Mary appears to have been no other than that famous public sinner, converted at the feet of Jesus. After her conversion she seems to have quit Magdala and have joined her sister Martha at Bethany to busy herself in the service of the Redeemer. There, at least, we find them together in our present narrative.

The castle of Bethany was near the great road that leads from Jericho to Jerusalem, fifteen stadia, or about a mile and a half from the latter city. Jesus had celebrated the Passover at Jerusalem, and it was probably in the last days of April of the year 27 that He approached Bethany to pay the two sisters a visit. But before we enter the castle, let us record the impressions a traveller received from this spot, so beloved by Heaven.

"Our journey stopped at Bethany. It was toward evening, when the bright light of the sun became milder and shadows began to lower. A solitary road leads from there to Mount Olive. Jerusalem disappears completely. Nothing is seen in the far distance but the mountains of Moab. I had imagined it thus. The spot is admirably suited to meditation and holy mystics. The noise of the world dies away at the approach of this solitude, neither the clamors of the multitudes nor the disputes of the priests and Scribes ever disturb its sacred silence. And one readily understands how Jesus, with preference, chose this pure and peaceful atmosphere."*)

In Gospel times, Bethany or Betheme — house of grace, — was truly the peaceful abode of friendship, such as can exist between kindred souls only. There is not the noisy crowd that usually followed Jesus; there is nothing that recalls the entertainments at Simon's or at Joseph of Arimathea's; even the Apostles seem to be absent, and if Lazarus is present, the fact is not mentioned. For, Jesus intended to consecrate that day exclusively to womankind, represented by these two sisters, so happy to have Him with them and so eager, each in her way, to

---

*) De Pressensé, "*Voyage au pays de l'Évangile.*"

manifest her joy about it to Him. Martha and Mary are the firstlings of that multitude of privileged women to whom Jesus, together with the gift of loving Him with a most delicate love, grants the happiness of His most familiar presence.

Nothing could be more contrary to the ideas and manners of the time than such a visit of the Saviour. We, accustomed as we are, to see the biblical narrative in the light of Christian customs, can hardly form an idea how extraordinary such a fact was in those days. But a feeling of admiration cannot fail to seize us, when, penetrating deeper into the conduct of the Saviour at this occasion, we find Him performing one of His radical cures in favor of the world's oppressed — woman.

For woman was, indeed, the most oppressed, and the Son of the "Woman" desires to be her Redeemer. This truth is commonplace, but it is always proper to re-iterate it, as there are women who separate from Christ and His Church through an abuse of that liberty which they enjoy only through Him.

The Gospel narrative of this particular

work of Redemption is of such simple and touching beauty that it singularly contrasts with the rigor of customs in that country and at that time.

"Now it came to pass as they went," says St. Luke,*) "that He entered into a certain town, and a certain woman named Martha received Him into her house. And she had a sister, called Mary, who sitting also at the Lord's feet heard His word."

The whole house had received an extra cleaning and polishing as soon as they had learned of the Saviour's coming, so that even the outward neatness reflected the inward purity of these two souls. Eagerly they now await Him. He arrives and enters the hospitable mansion. Now one should think that both with the same eagerness would listen to His words and enjoy those happy moments. But we are mistaken. Martha withdraws from the conversation; wholly assorbed by the preparations for the table and, to watch that all is done properly, she leaves the Saviour. Was it proper? Should earthly care have drawn her away when her God had approached so near?

---
*) Luke, X. 38, seq.

Mary gave the Saviour a better reception. On her knees, she listens intently to all His words; forgetful of His humanity, she contemplates His divinity. As formerly she had been in the abyss of crime, so now she seeks the summit of perfection.

Mary's position at the feet of the Saviour, according to Oriental custom, was nothing unusual, yet it must have a special meaning, else Holy Scripture would not mention it. And, indeed, that very attitude best becomes any woman, grateful for the teaching of Jesus; it likewise becomes the Christian woman as yet little advanced in Christian doctrine, and who but slowly progresses on the road to virtue and perfection. Mary, careful to avoid false teachers, wants to receive instruction from Him only Who is the Eternal Truth. How respectfully, how attentively does she listen!

The divine Teacher, by His example, shows us the duty, which His Church has always understood and practiced, of instructing woman in religious truths, to be zealously occupied about her advancement, and if need be, to advance her in secular science beyond the ordinary, in order to give a wider scope to her mind and heart.

As to Martha, she is feverishly occupied with the entertainment of the Saviour. But either from fatigue or from fear of not having everything as nice as she would like to have it, she approaches the divine guest and, with the liberty friendship gives, she says to Him:

"Lord, hast Thou no care that my sister hath left me alone to serve? Speak to her, therefore, that she help me."

"And the Lord, answering, saith to her: Martha, Martha, thou art careful, and art troubled about many things."

This answer, at first, will surprise us. If Martha is careful and troubled, it is for Him, and if she worries, it is to receive Him the better, and to show Him how much she esteems His visit. Yet evidently, hers was not the right manner, since Jesus disapproves of it. The divine goodness and eternal wisdom of Jesus will never approve of being carried away in His service too far, either by too much natural activity or by an agitation that disturbs the mind, even if our motives are the best. He wants serene and active souls, but they must remain in control of, and keep in harmony with, all their faculties and senses. Had not Mary one of those blessed hours that God reserves exclusively to Himself? At such a time all material work and earthly occupations must be subordinated to the demands of the spiritual life.

Trouble and worry are the every-day enemies that compromise the soul by the evil influence they exercise upon its common sense and reason, without which there can be no perfect virtue. Martha, indeed, was troubled. She is about to address an indirect reproach even to Jesus: "Dost Thou not see I have to do all the work by myself?" Such is lowest human nature, painted true to nature, such is frequently the first movement of wounded self-love. Martha thinks her guest pays no attention whatever to her or her labor. She covets a little praise, and she would like to see her sister busy in the kitchen instead of being entertained by Jesus.

Martha, thou art unjust towards the guest thou intendest to serve. Without looking at thee, He knows what thou art doing and keeps an account of thy labors. The eyes and the blessing of the Divine Friend are steadily on those who work for Him in any way. They are on the servant in the kitchen, on the laborer in the field or shop, on the writer in his study, on the soldier on the battlefield, no less than on the pious soul on her knees in the sanctuary. All He requires of us is the earnest will to act according to His intention.

"Martha, Martha," says Jesus, rebuking her for her incorrect ideas and imperfect sentiments, expressing, at the same time, the greatest cordiality in the repeated name, "but one thing is necessary."

The danger connected with excessive material labor consists in making us forget our soul; and material progress, sought for exclusively and at any price, brings about moral decadence. "The increase of wealth," says Le Play, "begets corruption, if it is not counterbalanced by a steady practice of the moral law." Moreover — and this is the key for the solution of the important social question — true material progress cannot be had except on condition of seeking first justice and charity by the total observance of the Gospel: Faith, Commandments, and Sacraments. Outside of this practice, both rich and poor become corrupt; statesmen find but deceptive systems, workingmen, but suffering and servitude, and the whole world will end by being in the tortures of merciless hatred and sterile constitutions.

By giving Martha a familiar lesson on this very humble subject, Jesus teaches all mankind, and makes known the absolutely essential and first principle of every social science: "Seek ye first the kingdom of God and His justice, and all the rest shall be added unto you" — on condition, that is, of making use of common sense and personal labor.

After this mild rebuke to Martha, Jesus continues to instruct Mary, who "has chosen the better part."—But, Lord, what merit can she claim for it? Hast not rather Thou chosen her for the contemplation of thy mysteries?

To be sure, Jesus calls first; and one's vocation is nothing else but the divine call by the hidden but strong voice which reverberates within the soul — our conscience; yet, when here the Saviour praises Mary for her choice, He does so, because she was free to refuse or accept the call. Such is also our merit when grace moves us. Mary had answered fully the advances of the Master; instead of distracting or absorbing herself in material objects, that subdue the soul by captivating the senses, she had concentrated her whole self in God. The more we hear of the Word of God, the more we long to hear still more of it, and the more we contemplate it, the more He will show us His adorable love and light, that will enlighten and inflame us. Perfect union with God requires silence.

By His visit to Mary and Martha Jesus elevates woman to this eminent state and this perfect love. To be attentive to God in order to unite with Him in heart and spirit, is an act of supreme perfection.

Humble, silent, with that intense look that is more expressive than words, in that quiet contemplation that surpasses all action, Mary remains at the feet of Jesus in adoration; her body is immovable, impregnated with celestial light, and her soul soars towards the Saviour. Lo, they are united! Behold her enraptured by truth and love, drinking in eagerly the happiness of Heaven!

Nevertheless, human life cannot be spent in celestial contemplation, even by those who have "chosen the better part." Material activity must necessarily interrupt the hours of high flight and of heart-to-heart communion with God.

Those most elevated by the grace of Heaven have to busy themselves, at times, with the lowly things of earth. Mary cannot get along without the labor of Martha, as little as Martha can dispense herself from close recollection in God, like Mary.

Thus, considering them together, in the union of their activities, Martha and Mary represent the vocation of all men, even of the most perfect. The union of these activities constitutes the spiritual life that each of us should feel bound to lead, after the example of Jesus Christ. Spiritual life is not the exclusive endowment of the cloister; in varying degrees, according to the designs of divine Providence, it must be that of all Christians without exception. Nor is perfection incompatible with outside labor. If all men are not in possession of the "better part" in the absolute sense of the word, all may have a beautiful part, for all are visited by Jesus, who becomes their guest in Holy Communion.

Let us women take care not to forget that to one of us the Saviour gave the most important of His teachings! He did it that we might practice it and that others might learn it by our example. By the will of God, woman, at the domestic hearth, is to teach Christian recollection and continuously preach "the one thing necessary", that of "the better part."

# THE WOMAN UNDER A SPIRIT OF INFIRMITY.

### JESUS STRAIGHTENS HER.

WHEN one Sabbath day Jesus was teaching in the synagogue, "behold there was a woman who had a spirit of infirmity eighteen years; and she was bowed together, neither could she look upwards at all."*)

Especially on Sabbath and holidays Jesus used to teach in the synagogue. Sick and healthy people flocked thither to obtain favors from Him.

But was it lawful to heal on the Sabbath

---

*) Luke, XIII. 11 seq.

day? That question had become a subject of never-ending discussions between the doctors and Pharisees. Was it allowed to care for the sick on that day? Even here the schools of Hillel and Schammai were divided. The dominant opinion was, that caring for the sick was allowed in case of imminent death only. When a man had been buried under a fallen building, according to the Talmud, it was allowed to remove enough of the debris to let him breathe, but no more.

Hence scandal and dissensions arose from each new cure the Saviour performed on a Sabbath. Hence also those wily questions the zealots of the Law put so frequently to Him, not to be instructed, but to confound Him before His disciples and the people. Under just such circumstances the Saviour found occasion to speak about Sabbath observance, — not only to answer the queries of His adversaries but also to explain the third book of Moses, that happened to be read that day.

Now, about all things Jesus had spoken with an authority that excited the admiration of others. By His humane doctrine and extreme goodness He practically condemned those cruel teachings, imposed upon the people as divine laws by their Pharisaic masters and teachers. The poor and simple-minded, the unfortunate and sick never wearied of listening to Him. They loved in Him their protector, their friend and Saviour.

However, the woman "bowed together" does not seem to have come to the synagogue for the purpose of being cured by Jesus; perhaps, she had never before met the "great prophet", and knew nothing of Him except the contradictory reports current about Him. But as a religious woman and a faithful observer of the Law, she does not consider her disease an excuse for missing divine service. Doubtless she had tried medical help, but in vain, and now she has come to the conclusion that she is incurable and that death alone will relieve her. For who, after all, could straighten that body bent to the earth? Who could enable her to lift up her eyes again to Heaven?

And behold, all of a sudden, before she has prostrated herself before the invisible majesty of Jehova, she is face to face with the Saviour.

Woman, He is there for all, but for thee in particular. Instead of going nearer to Him, thou remainest at a distance, asking nothing of Him Who can do all. Hence Jesus is to look after thee first, and thou, standing aside, stooping and full of fear, art called by Him.

"Whom when Jesus saw, He called her to Him, and said to her: Woman, thou art delivered from thy infirmity. And He laid His hands upon her, and immediately she was made straight, and glorified God."

"And the ruler of the synagogue (being angry that Jesus had healed on the Sabbath) answering said to the multitude: Six days there are wherein you ought to work. In them, therefore, come and be healed; and not on the Sabbath day."

Not daring to blame the Saviour directly, the Rabbi rebukes the woman. Time and again, the Redeemer had proved, by word and deed, that the Pharisaic rigor was contrary to the true spirit of the Law, and that works of mercy and compassion are quite compatible with the holiness of the Lord's day. He undertakes it once more.

"Ye hypocrites," He said to them, "does

not every one of you on the Sabbath day loose his ox or his ass from the manger, and lead them to water? And ought not this daughter of Abraham, whom Satan has bound, lo, these eighteen years, be loosed from this bond on the Sabbath day?" And when He had said these things, His adversaries were ashamed, but "all the people rejoiced for all the things that were gloriously done."

They were condemned, these false zealots of the Law, these oppressors of men of good will. No worse tyranny can be imagined than the burden placed on the neck of the humble in the name of God and of the Law by the pride of these false doctors. But the most simple word, inspired by a righteous and benevolent heart, is able to dumfound the hypocritical scribes.

"Do you mean," Jesus meant to say, "that you take less care of your sick brethren than of your animals?"

May we not look upon this physical disease of the woman as a true picture of all those in despair? Is it not likewise an allegoric type of scruples and fears that bind the soul?

There is an intelligent, well-founded fear,

which is the salutary effect of a previous fall or of the consideration of the divine justice. This fear is numbered among the gifts of the Holy Ghost; and, although it is not the whole wisdom itself, i. e., perfect love, it is the beginning of it, either because it gradually leads to it, or because, united with repentance, it forms part of the love that begins. In either case it is a boon.

But as, in the physical world, one organ often thrives and develops at the expense of another, so, in the realm of the soul, one affection may overpower another. Most certainly, repentance is good; but if grief for the past is carried to excess, it may shroud the soul in darkest gloom and reduce it to a state of pusilanimity. Such a soul cares little for instruction, loses the power of discerning good from evil, and lacks personal and strong impulses to act, particularly in public, of which there is such need in this century of indecision and doubt.

Who, then, is that Christian with the sad and careworn look? Should he open his heart to you and allow you to penetrate into the sorrowful solitude of his soul, you would find him in the clutches of servile fear. This fear, once so salutary to rouse him from his spiritual lethargy, when sin had killed the life of his soul, now is a positive evil for him, paralyzing and shrouding him in darkness. Christian, forget thy evil days, see the ray of light that enlightened thee, the pardon that thy repentance called down, and the mercy of thy God! What hast thou to fear, beloved and hundredfold redeemed soul? Hast thou no confidence whatever in God who pardoned thee and called thee to partake of His own flesh and blood? . . .

It is useless to admonish those unfortunate beings stooping to the earth, unable to lift up their eyes to Heaven. Not even the most authoritative voice, the voice of God's representative, can convince them that, no matter how numerous or grievous their sins may have been, God's mercy is greater and always ready to forgive. And it is extremely hard to make them understand that, with the help of God's grace the act of contrition annihilates sin, and if that contrition was perfect, anticipated even the absolution granted in the Sacrament of Penance.

Sinner of yesterday, fix thy eyes upon the stooping woman, and ask thy Saviour to heal thee also of thy pusilanimity. He can do it. Should He delay, should the remembrance of thy sins continue to rest heavily on thee and almost suffocate thee, accept it as a penance — it is, indeed, a heavy one — be consoled by the thought of suffering, and do not stoop lower still for fear of not seeing thy divine consoler when He passes near thee.

No less manifest is here the intention of the Saviour to alleviate and elevate the social condition of woman. He wants her to enter upon a life of religious and social activity. Therefore He called her that was infirm, stooping, stiff, and, although a daughter of Abraham, bound by Satan since eighteen years; and, for a manifest sign of her deliverance, places His hands upon her, saying: "Woman, thou art delivered from thy infirmity." And immediately she stands erect and praises God for the wonderful cure.

From that moment she, too, is called to act in public: to accept and assimilate in herself the Spirit of Truth That delivers and saves, and to serve the Lord by communicating of this divine Spirit to the enthusiastic people surrounding Him and make them proclaim aloud this prodigy and their joy over it.

Henceforth, woman is to take part in the work of restoration and salvation, first, of herself, and then, of her own sex, that in future shall share with the other the same redeeming graces, the same ameliorations, the same terrestrial progress contained in the divine words which shall never cease to germinate and grow in all ages and climes.

This straightening of woman under a spirit of infirmity, that, unsolicited, Jesus here performs by a special and positive act of His divine will, He had begun already in the earliest days of His public life. One might be tempted to say, He now hastens to the accomplishment of this particular work of Redemption. Woman, lifted by Jesus from the mire, thou shalt, through Him, become the upholder and defender of human dignity; henceforth thou shalt be esteemed and respected, and frequently shall the radiant aureola of sanctity encircle thy brow. This transformation offers one of the most lovely spectacles on earth. Behold the Christian woman at work, henceforth, to relieve all poor, stooping and suffering beings.*)

---

*) To understand this relief work of woman better, cast a glance at the Orient, where millions of women,

Did not a slave become a queen of France, and as a great queen—because she was a great

by law and custom, are stooping in a degradation of which we have but a faint idea. Whilst the world tends towards unity, or rather uniform modernity, whilst Orient and Occident rapidly approach each other, and whilst the nations of Asia assimilate to themselves our material progress, woman has no share in this immense movement of interests and struggles. She remains in her abjection. Even under French dominion, the Mohamedan woman continues to be treated as a beast, less esteemed than a horse, and sold for less money. (According to Kabylian law, the father may sell his daughter, the husband, his wife, and both may be deprived of all rights, including inheritance.) She is still the unfortunate, stooping woman under the monstrous despotism of man, which finds its most revolting expression in the harem. "By it the Orient subsists, and by it it will end. But when? Soon, were not the Occident infected with scepticism, armed with all physical forces, but free from moral restraint." Listen, at least, to the 100,000 victims of Armenia, of whom those are most to be pitied that were not throttled. "Courage fails to retrace the revolting picture of these abominations that surpass in turpitude anything imagination can invent."

"Having satisfied their beastly passions, these monsters with a human face take advantage of the despair and gloom of their unfortunate victims to force them to a denial of their faith." (The Rev. F. Charmetant.)

Listen also to the touching complaints of those other victims: "How happy you, Christian women, must feel," one day a Mohamedan said to the wife of a

## The Woman under a Spirit of Infirmity. 133

saint—accomplish marvels of deliverance and progress? Let us imitate her.*)

---

Christian physician at Constantinopel, "you go where you please; for us going out would be exposing ourselves to death." — "How can you," said a Kabyl woman to a sister on the African missions, "how can you, European women, get out?" (*Annals of the Work of Mary Immaculate*, March, 1896.)

Yes, we are happy and privileged, because we live among Christian nations, hence we should unite against this terrible injustice, this shameful sore in the side of humanity. Christian women, watch with more attention the sufferings of your heathen sisters! Let us form a crusade, not alone of prayers, but by giving our gold and our hearts to this work of deliverance, so valiantly kept up since the apostolic times by the missionaries of both sexes. A more special work for the deliverance of heathen women, groaning under the most humiliating despotism, is established at Paris under the patronage of Mary Immaculate and claims our help.

*) Bathilda, a widow with three children, showed herself the "valiant woman" of the Scriptures, and manfully assumed the regency. She sought a counterbalance against the feudal system in the backing of the people and clergy; she abolished the old Roman polltax, lowered the taxes in general,—a rare venture; and still under the impression of the painful past, she forbade to expose infants, or to introduce Christian captives on French territory; she redeemed a great number of slaves, provided liberally for the poor of all classes, founded the abbey of Corby, enlarged Chelles, enriched Luxeuil and a hundred others; she called

Like other Bathildas, like the women of the Gospel, these Christian women glorify God and make others glorify Him, when they are busying themselves in the service of the Master, joyfully, reasonably, possessing worldly and religious knowledge, and understanding their domestic and social duties.

But when women pass their lives in idleness, or fill them only with futile labors, though free from faults and, so to say, innocent, they most certainly are a failure. They as Christians ought to know that it is not enough to fear sin, to weep over one's faults,

---

into her crown-council the illustrious St. Leger, bishop of Autun, the future formidable adversary of the terrible Ebroin, and several other bishops. Even outside of her dominion she made the name of the Franks respected as well as law and justice. The king of Lombardy had rejected his wife and was about to introduce Arianism into his kingdom, when she brought him to repentance by her ambassador. The proud Rotharis bowed his head before this former slave, transfigured by the double crown of royalty and sanctity. When she saw her task fulfilled and her sons grown up, deeply affected by the death of St. Eloi, her intimate guide, and beholding the intestine quarrels that threatened to destroy her admirable plan of French unity, she withdrew into a convent, to consecrate herself entirely to God, as before she had given herself entirely to her people." (Lecoy de la Marche, "La Fondation de la France.")

to abstain from evil, but that they must act in the midst of the crowd at a time when human life more and more becomes a life of public struggles.

They ought to know their duty goes beyond the limits of personal piety and a pusilanimous devotion, if they want to have any influence over a society that is led away from God. Yes, placing their confidence in Christ, let them boldly march forward as apostles of activity. In that way they shall do the work of God; in that way, too, even without their knowledge, they shall straighten the hearts "bowed together under a spirit of infirmity."

"For you have not received the spirit of bondage again in fear, but you have received the spirit of adoption, wherewith we cry: Abba (Father)." \*)

And wherever dwells the Spirit of the Lord, there is also true liberty.

---

\*) Rom., VIII. 15.

# MARTHA AND MARY.

**JESUS RESUSCITATES THEIR BROTHER.**

ESUS had left Jerusalem and crossed the Jordan to avoid the snares His enemies had laid for Him at the capital. About that time Lazarus fell sick at Bethany.

Thereupon his sisters, Martha and Mary, sent a messenger to Jesus with the delicate and discreet message:

"Lord, behold, he whom Thou lovest is sick." *)

They thought it sufficient to let Jesus know the condition of their brother; yet, contrary to their expectation, this news

---
*) John, XI.

## Martha and Mary.

seemed to make no impression on Him and He simply answered: "This sickness is not unto death but for the glory of God: that the Son of God may be glorified by it."

And He remained two days longer in the same place. For Martha and Mary it was a strange absentation and a painful expectation. He Who by a single word could have healed their dear brother, did not seem to will it. The Supreme Consoler seemed to abandon His friends to their bereavement and sorrow. The Evangelist himself is astonished at it, for he cannot help repeating: "Now Jesus loved Martha, and her sister Mary, and Lazarus." The Saviour let affliction reach its highest degree in the death of Lazarus, though He had given as a reason for the affliction of His friends, "that sickness is for the glory of God." To procure the glory of God He had come into the world; and now the sufferings, the agony, and the death of Lazarus shall give the most beautiful testimony to the Christ of the living God.

Thus Lazarus died, far away from his friend. Then Jesus said to His disciples: "Let us go into Judea again, Lazarus, our friend is dead, and I am glad for your sake, that you may believe."

God disposes events not only for His glory, which they always manifest, but also for the benefit of men, as any one may see who is attentive to His word and knows how to consider facts in their true relations.

Disciples of the Lord, behold here the value of your faith! That you may have a faith capable of transplanting mountains, which, in your future actions and sufferings, shall be both a light and a force to you, He lets Lazarus die and silences His own sorrow.

Similar dispositions of divine Providence are still, and will always be, of frequent occurrence. Hence the necessity of knowing how to await the hour of God without despair and murmuring; but those more perfect, at such times, bend their knees to adore the inscrutable decrees of Providence and pray with the Saviour: Thy will be done...... The future, often already on earth, but certainly in Heaven, shall reveal the reasons of so many secret trials and of the apparent failures of so many prayers.

"Lazarus is dead," said our Lord to His disciples, "because I was not there, but let us go to him."

What a touching insinuation! Had I been

there, my friend, I would not have been able to see thee suffer thus, nor to let thee die.— When God permits our tears to flow, it seems He was not there, He must needs turn away His eyes and ears, so much He loves us. But soon He shall return and reward us for our sorrow and affliction. Blessed are they that weep!

Jesus wants to see our tears, that, like prayers, ascend to Heaven and bring about His return, as did those of His friends at Bethany.

"Let us go to him!" said the Master. And Thomas, who knew the danger of a return into Judea, said to his fellow disciples: "Let us also go, that we may die with Him."

Indeed, His return to Jerusalem exposed the Saviour anew to all the open and secret attacks of the Pharisees, who were resolved to kill Him, and, perhaps, also His disciples. From the beginning, the disciples of Christ had cared for the sick, the afflicted and the poor, sacrificing their own comfort, and wealth, often endangering their lives in the service of their neighbor. And the thanks they received were open or secret persecutions until this very day. In France, a set of

Masonic hypocrites, by an iniquitous law, strives to suppress all Religious Orders by slow degrees. The Radicals of Ecuador drove them into exile by force, and their Mexican "brethren" are so scared of these angels of charity that they will not allow any convent on Mexican soil.

A great number of distinguished Jews surrounded the two sisters at Bethany, who, according to custom, sat on the floor, with torn vestments, veiled heads, and bare feet. Around them, forming a circle, we see their relatives and friends and hired mourners. The prescribed silence is not interrupted except by sobbings and groanings, that are to last seven days after the three days of weeping are over.

The Jews buried their dead usually two or three hours after their demise. The burial place was ordinarily a cave or an excavation in the rock. The corpses were embalmed and wrapt up in winding sheets after the manner of the Egyptians. The rich, accompanied by relatives and friends, or at least ten hired mourners, also visited the sepulchre and renewed their lamentations. These funeral visits were continued until the body was decomposed.

Martha and Mary went through the whole ceremonial, but their hearts were with Him Who had not come.

Finally He arrives, but Lazarus was already buried four days. Martha learns of the Saviour's arrival first. Seized with emotion, the long mourning veil on her head, she runs to meet Him: "Lord, if Thou hadst been here, my brother had not died."

She manifests no reproach, but the certainty of Jesus' all powerful intercession and the sorrowful conviction, that, had He been present, He would not have let Lazarus die. A remarkable coincidence — the same thought had passed through the mind of the Master — attesting the perfect harmony existing between Him and His friends.

Jesus said to her: "Thy brother shall rise again."

Martha said to Him: "I know that he shall rise again in the resurrection at the last day." Confused by sorrow, she does not seem to understand the precise meaning of these words, which answered so well to her secret desire; perhaps she did not dare to entertain such a sweet hope — it would be too much happiness.

But Jesus wants to grant it, hence, He says to her:

"I am the Resurrection and the Life: he that believeth in me, although he be dead, shall live. And every one that liveth, and believeth in me, shall not die forever. Believest thou this?"

Jesus reveals Himself here as the Master of Life, a doctrine He had as yet taught to no one. Lo, woman who is to suffer most by separation on earth, receives the certain and consoling truth that we shall meet again in Heaven. She, whom the doctors and philosophers despised, is the first to behold in the divine light the mysteries of death.

And here the Saviour speaks as the Son of God, equal to the Father: "I am the Resurrection and the Life."

And He adds: "Dost thou believe this?"

"Yes, Lord," she answers, "I have believed that Thou art Christ, the Son of the living God."

Spontaneously Martha makes this profession of faith, that same profession which brought Peter the supreme pastorship of the Church. This profession of faith is the necessary preparation for the apostolic mission with which woman is to be charged, and it is, above all, the condition under which the Saviour is to perform the resuscitation of Lazarus. Thus consoled by Him Who is "the Resurrection and the Life," Martha hastens to call Mary — secretly, not knowing what Jesus had come for, and fearing to displease Him, should she bring the crowd along. And she said to her sister:

"The Master is come and calleth for thee."

The Friend had made a long journey to see these sisters, and now in turn, He does not deprive them of the duty and the satisfaction of hastening toward Him. Had Mary known the arrival of Jesus, she would not have been able to check her impetuosity nor to wait for such a happy message.

"For Jesus was not come into the town, but was still in the place, where Martha had met Him," waiting for the sisters. As the house of Martha and Mary was filled with acquaintances, relations, and friends, drawn there by the mourning at that rich and opulent mansion, Jesus, from motives of delicacy and friendship, desired an intimate conversation with His friends in sorrow. "There is a certain secret," says

Bossuet, "between Jesus and interior souls, such as represented by Mary. One has to enter into, but not disturb, that secret by mixing it with worldly alloy."

And then, was it not too painful for Thee, O Son of Man, to enter that dear mansion at Bethany, once so full of joy, when Thy friends celebrated Thy return, but now filled with sorrow? Indeed, such a feeling was not unworthy of Thy heart, and more and more we shall understand that on earth Thou sharest all human feelings.

"The Jews therefore that were with her in the house and comforted her, when they saw Mary that she rose up speedily and went out, followed her, saying: She goes to the grave to weep there." It was a sacred custom with the Jews to accompany their relatives to the grave. Hence they followed her, but at a distance, since no Jew accompanied a woman nor spoke to her in public.

"When Mary therefore was come where Jesus was, seeing Him, she fell at His feet, and saith to Him: Lord, if Thou hadst been here, my brother would not have died."

She neither had any complaint nor reproach to make; her heart moved her to say: "O Lord and Father, in Whom is our trust, I come to offer Thee the shreds of this heart, all filled with Thy glory, which Thou hast deigned to tear."

And Jesus asks for no more. That speechless heart speaks louder than words. Mary utters but that one sentence, and it is enough.

"Blessed be Thou, O Lord Jesus, for having willed that we should know the tenderness Thou hast for Thy friends. May we imitate it, and love after Thy example. Hearts of flint are not the hearts that please Thee." (Bossuet.)

"Jesus therefore, when He saw her weeping, and the Jews that were come with her weeping, groaned in spirit and troubled Himself. And said: Where have you laid Him?" — Holy groaning of the Son of God! Blessed trouble of the Son of Man! Jesus, for us Thou passest through our funeral hours; in Thee reverberates the sobbing of our sorrows that find appeasement but in Thee!

"They answered: Lord come and see!" Then Jesus went to the grave and — wept.

He will not weep when, delivered to His enemies, He is maltreated and crucified; He had wept but once before when, in sight of the guilty city and its polluted Temple, He thought of the horrible chastisement awaiting it. But this moment, He weeps with Martha and Mary to consecrate our mourning and the bonds of friendship.

"The Jews therefore said: Behold how He loved him. But some of them said: Could not He that opened the eyes of the man born blind, have caused that this man should not die?"

Thus spoke the multitude, each according to his own heart — well or ill — but none ever thought, much less said: Can He not recall him to life?

"Jesus therefore, again groaning in Himself, cometh to the sepulchre."

But, Lord, why dost Thou groan again? Is it because before Thy eyes is the picture of the human race plunged in evil, surrounded by horrors, having succumbed to the universal death of sin? Or because Thou also seest those that are dead for all eternity? And who knows but He may on this occasion have seen, too, the horrors of His own death upon the cross?

According to the Jewish regulations, cemeteries were at some distance from the dwellings of men. Here lay the corpse of Lazarus, in a cave over which a heavy stone was rolled. "Jesus said: Take away the stone. Martha, the sister of him that was dead, said to Him: Lord, by this time he stinketh, for he is of four days."

"Jesus said to her: Did not I say to thee, if thou believe, thou shalt see the glory of God? They took therefore away the stone. And Jesus lifting up His eyes said: Father, I give Thee thanks that Thou hast heard me. And I know that Thou hearest me always, but because of the people who stand about have I said it; that they may believe that Thou hast sent me."

Jesus looking up to Heaven, takes Heaven for a witness that He is the Messiah, the Son of God, and gives thanks to His heavenly Father. This prayer, recited in the hearing of the multitude, in that solemn hour, is an evident proof that not alone His word is true, but that He Himself is the Word, by Whom all things were made and by Whom even beings that are no more can come back to life.

"When He had said these things, He cried with a loud voice: Lazarus, come forth! And presently he that had been dead came forth, bound feet and hands with winding bands and his face was bound about with a napkin."

Fear and awe had overwhelmed all present to such a degree that no one had the courage to approach the resuscitated man. Martha herself makes no rush towards the beloved brother to free him from his bands; Jesus has to give the command to take them off: "Loose him," He said, "and let him go."

"Loose him!" — A significant word! Jesus Christ has restored him to life, but He makes use of intermediaries to have the bands of Lazarus removed. Soon the day shall be on hand, when from Heaven above He shall utter the words of resurrection to sinners, whilst His Apostles on earth give absolution and thereby remove the bandages of sin.

Martha, Mary, lead away your brother! Lead him home, whilst from your hearts, filled with perfect happiness, you pour out praise and adoration and thanksgiving to Jesus; and, then, give way to joy and gratitude at this incomparable feast of friendship!

Nowhere did Jesus show Himself more fully, nowhere did He show His human feelings in such close touch with His infinite power. So it is still that, by secret divine, the most trying afflictions provoke the most brilliant manifestations of divine friendship. The deepest sorrows are frequently rooted in the most merciful designs of our Saviour. To make us more compassionate and charitable, He permits, at times, that we suffer and feel unhappy. Yet He keeps watch with the same divine heart that to the sisters at Bethany granted the resurrection of their dear, lamented brother.

# THE WIDOW'S MITE.

EARLY in the morning of the last Tuesday passed by Him on earth, Jesus left Bethany to ascend to Jerusalem. An eager crowd awaited Him at the Temple, where, without any interference, He had been teaching the previous evening. But His enemies were incessantly plotting how to lay hands on His person, since they had tried in vain to ruin Him in the eyes of the people. No time was to be lost; the enthusiasm of the multitudes for Him was growing steadily. Had they not cheered Him after the resurrection of Lazarus in the very streets of Jerusalem and in the sight of the Temple? No prophet ever enjoyed such an honor. We must do

## The Widow's Mite. 151

away with "this seducer." Thus thought and spoke the Pharisees.

Now, to warn for a last time all men of good will against the hypocrisy of His enemies, Jesus pronounced the solemn maledictions against them. That passionate and painful discourse had fatigued Him. Suffering of the soul quickly exhausts our vital forces. But what must not have been the sufferings of Him Who came to bring light and peace and found but obstinacy and opposition?

Jesus had gone to the upper terrace of the Temple, called the Holy. Before He descended to the vestibule, He took a seat in the part of the Lord's House accessible to women, opposite the alms-box. Three boxes, named "Shoferoth" from their trumpetlike orifices, were surrounded by the crowd: Jews of all tribes and of all conditions put in their alms, some modestly, others ostentatiously. Jesus observed them silently...... God thus regards our religious actions, scrutinizes our motives, and notes our generosity. But as all those that passed before the eyes of Jesus did not notice Him, so we frequently fail to see the eye of God that is always over us, because we are so little accustomed to heavenly things and so little prepared to perceive invisible realities.

Jesus beheld how the people cast money into the treasury, "and many that were rich cast in much."*)

Many, i. e., the greater number of the people, give willingly. They fulfil the duty imposed on every man, to render part of the earthly goods bestowed upon him by God to his heavenly Giver. As at the time of Jesus, so in our days, this duty is incumbent on all. God places Himself, as it were, at the mercy and good will of His creatures. All are overwhelmed with His favors, but those that love Him, feel happy in offering of their own free will from among His own gifts; nor are they jealous, but rejoice when they see others offer more or richer gifts than their own.

Suddenly, Jesus interrupts the silence. Eyes of Jesus, what has surprised you? Silence of Jesus, what can interrupt thee?

It is a poor woman: "And there came a certain poor widow and she cast in two mites, which make a farthing."**)

---
*) Mark, XII. 41—44.
**) The smallest Jewish coin, about half a cent.

Widow and poor, what a misfortune! This woman does not dispense herself from the legal alms; she gives what she can and more than she ought.

Christian women, poor and suffering, who modestly hide yourselves in the shadow of the church, see and hear what the Saviour is doing!

"Calling His disciples together, He saith to them: Amen, I say to you, this poor widow has cast in more than all they that cast into the treasury."

Never before had the Saviour called His disciples together in such an explicit manner to admire something. This something must, therefore, be very beautiful, O Lord, that Thy own admiration is not sufficient, but that Thou carest to share it with Thy friends!

To admire what is good, is a salutary and beautiful sentiment in the midst of so much jealousy and detraction, that we cannot help rejoicing to see it honored by the example of Him Who is the "Light and the Truth." "Amen I say to you, this poor widow has given more than all others; for all they did cast in of their abundance, but she of her want cast in all she had, even her whole living."

Surprising words of Jesus! How can I who have nothing give more than they who have much? Yet it is possible, since God Himself teaches it, for the great consolation of the humble and poor, to whom it cannot be repeated too often; to give of one's poverty and for God's sake to suffer greater privation, is proof of very rare, but also very deep, religious sentiment. And when we take into consideration that this act of supreme generosity is accomplished by a poor widow, who, after the custom of those days, was not allowed to earn a living, but was doomed to servitude and exposed without any protection to those Scribes and Pharisees that, in the words of the Saviour, "devour the houses of the widows", we cannot help admiring and blessing the divine and human praise lavished on one belonging to the class of the "disinherited." And doubtless, it was not an isolated act of hers; for what constitutes the great value and the great beauty of virtuous deeds is their repetition. The will, for which the first act was perhaps a painful sacrifice, soon experiences its delights.

Are they, then, excusable who, under pretext of poverty, refuse to give alms, when their very poverty enables them to "give more"? It is a grand donation that the factory or hired girl makes in the shape of a quarter or half a dollar for the church or the school, or when she lays aside her weekly contribution for the propagation of the faith. It means "giving more" when the poor laboring woman, who depends on the work of her hands for a living, takes the time to instruct a child in the religious duties, or embroiders the alb to be used by the priest at the altar. They also give richly who divide their bread with the needy, or wear patched and mended clothing in order to cover the nakedness of others.

And, in another order, they give richly who secretly offer their sufferings to God for the conversion of sinners and the deliverance of the poor souls in purgatory; or who forget their own sorrow to alleviate the pains of others..... You who practice these things, rejoice! God looks down upon you and admires you; for above all He is the Friend of the humble and the Father of the poor and despised. Do you see how, here on earth already, He is occupied about them, how He defends and glorifies them, and unceasingly recommends them to His disciples, saying: "Whatever is done to the least of my brethren is done to me"? In a sublime manner He shows His predilection for the multitude of unfortunates, women in particular. Those, dear Jesus, who are animated by Thy spirit, who have Thy heart, know it, and everywhere on earth try to imitate Thee, whilst Thy enemies think of nothing but how to lead the multitude, always a prey to their own vices and the dupes of exploiting charlatans, unto perdition. Thy friends, in order to follow Thee, occupy themselves quite differently.

In spite of nineteen hundred years of clamoring against it, the Law of the Gospel is so imposing and sublime that, of late, an infidel could not help rendering this supreme tribute to it: "The Gospel makes no class distinctions between the souls of men, and the most humble are lifted up by what for them is the highest good; tenderness and esteem. The Gospel is the epopee of the simple, an anticipated hymn from the Jerusalem of the poor and the miserable."\*)

---

\*) Challemel Lacour, Academic Speech of Sept. 25, 1894.

The eyes of the Saviour, the same loving and compassionate eyes that singled out the mite of the widow, are still on all who are abandoned here below.

# MARY MAGDALEN.

**JESUS DEFENDS HER AGAINST HIS DISCIPLES.**

ON the first day of the month Nisan, or the eighth of April 29, Jesus left Jericho with the caravan going to Jerusalem. He went to Bethany, where He arrived towards evening. For the last time He wished to pass a few moments of real, though sad, peace in the beloved circle of his friends who feel uneasy on account of the animosities which menace Him all around. He desires to receive from Martha and Mary and Lazarus the last testimonials of an attachment whose beauty Heaven and earth admire. He is willing, however, to take the solemn Sabbath supper at Simon's, where the inhabitants of Bethany wish to offer it to Him, in thanksgiving for all His benefits, and especially for the resurrection of Lazarus. It was the Master's first stay among them since that great event, and the desire to show Him their attachment and admiration and to feast Him, was the more natural, since on account of the miracle performed on Lazarus, He had been excommunicated by the Sanhedrin.*)

At this banquet, Lazarus was one of the guests of honor. His presence was the most palpable proof of the almighty power of Jesus and an emphatic protest against His persecutors.

"Six days before the pasch," says St. John, "Jesus arrived at Bethany where Lazarus had been dead, whom Jesus raised to life. And they made Him a supper there..... Lazarus was one of them that were at table with Him."

---

\*) The inhabitants of Bethany were so attached to the Saviour that for His sake they, too, were persecuted, and Bethany destroyed by the Jews, out of hatred against Jesus. They were accused of placing themselves above the Law. (John, XII. 1—8; Mark, XIV, 3—9; Matt., XXVI, 6—13.)

We can easily picture to ourselves the large banquet hall, ornamented and decorated with tapestry and flowers; cushions were placed along the table for the numerous guests, who cannot look often enough at Lazarus and express their astonishment at beholding alive him, whose death had filled Bethany and Jerusalem with painful emotion. Among the visitors and guests the Twelve were dispersed. Their hearts were heavy with the sad predictions of their Master. Did they not know too well the hatred of His enemies?

Women are admitted for the service only. Martha is there with her usual ardor and vivacity. As true friends of Jesus, they readily recognize that He is in need of other manifestations of attachment besides theirs; they are pleased to see so many honoring Him and they feel happy to be able to assist. "Martha served." The Saviour occupied the place of honor. Mildness shone from His serene eyes, and ineffable beauty from His face.

"But, lo! Mary enters the banquet hall, the rich and stately Mary, the former public sinner. She now stands before Him Who rehabilitated and justified her by His divine pardon. She is no longer the woman whose youth and beauty barely cover the shame of vice and who trembling approaches the feet of Jesus, as a servant, to shed tears there and dry them. Three years of grace have passed over her brow and sanctity now sheds lustre around her person.*")

"And when Jesus was in Bethany, in the house of Simon the Leper, there came to Him a woman having an alabaster box of precious ointment and poured it on His head as He was at table."

Why that, Mary? Why not stay with your sister, busied with domestic cares? Can it be that women have a higher vocation than looking after the corporal wants and the material welfare of the Saviour? Is it not enough for her, out of love for Jesus, to be the mother and servant of the Apostles? Does it not suffice that she fill her hands with good works in His name? Certainly not! Mary, here, is about to crown all by adding to the services already rendered the cult of perfect love toward Jesus. She is not content to love silently, she wants to announce it aloud that

---

*) Lacordaire, "Life of Mary Magdalen."

she loves Him. True love must find its outward expression. Hence Mary makes known her love as she feels it. She pours perfume over the feet that went in search of her; she pours it over His forehead whose thoughts of Redemption had taught her her own mission and destiny; she anoints the Chief Who is soon to be torn to pieces by the ingratitude of men, and Who, never ceasing in all centuries, to feel new thorns and to be harried by new denials, shall one day receive no other honors than those rendered Him by woman.

But sublime ideas and beautiful actions always find detractors. Only few men understand them. Here on earth, admiration will continue to be the rarest as well as the most exquisite sentiment. "And His disciples, seeing this, had indignation, saying: To what purpose is this waste? For this might have been sold for much, and given to the poor."

Even the disciples begrudge the honor rendered to the God Who had lowered Himself to become their brother; to the Master Whom they were soon to lose; to the Friend Whose funeral was near. And for this woman, that loved Him Who loved them, and that, in their stead, came to render the homage which their masculine hands were unable to bestow, they had neither gratitude nor sympathy. They are not yet enlightened, instructed, and transformed. As yet their voice brings forth neither approval nor happiness.

Mediocrity, incapable of love, is likewise incapable of understanding love. It will slander and hate it; it condemns itself; and feeling the necessity of justifying its conduct, it invents pretexts and hides itself under the cloak of virtue.

"Why was not this ointment," said Judas Iscariot, "sold for three hundred pieces of silver and given to the poor?"

"Now he said so," adds the Evangelist, "not because he cared for the poor, but because he was a thief, and having the purse, carried the things contained therein."

Such is the truth . . . Judas had as little love for the poor as the misers, the egotists, or the epicures. Carried away by their passions, they have but one desire: to satisfy these passions; they count the money and calculate closely what amount of base gratification can be had from it. Three hundred pieces of silver — an immense sum! Judas very soon will sell His Master for ten times less!

What do they care if the house of the Lord appears empty, or falls into ruins? What is it to them that the sacred vestments are worn and threadbare? "Why this waste?" is their query. Do they know who He is that stays with us in the tabernacle? Do they, indeed, believe that the Host is alive, that the living Jesus is hidden under its appearance? Ah, Lord, we shall not have Thee always thus, we shall not always give Thee shelter among us, nor ornament Thy altars and surround Thee with generous and delicate attentions . . . . Life is short, fortune fickle; soon we may be unable to give Thee anything!

Up to this moment, the anxious and surprised guests had awaited the word of the Master, Who had kept silent so far. But now He intervenes, and that to defend the woman against the unjust and specious attacks of His disciples. Without blaming them directly, without even tearing the mask from the hypocrisy of Judas, confining Himself to combating the alleged reasons which had found but too many approvers, the Master says: "Let her alone, that she may keep it for the day of my burial. For the poor you have always with you, but me you have not always."

The infinitely good heart of Jesus puts into these words the whole meekness of His spirit. Jesus, grant us to listen to Thee, to penetrate into Thy divine tenderness, to understand Thy friendship!

We cannot reflect too much on it: our Lord has no hard word, even for Judas. Far from confounding the wretches around Him, or teaching them the homage due Him, He forgets His own self entirely; and if He upraids them at all, He does it because they cause this woman trouble; and if He blames them, it is because they condemn her good deed.

Did Mary Magdalen comprehend the extent and the value of the act she performed? Compelled by her heart, moved by the Spirit from on high, she had, indeed, accomplished a symbolical action, the import of which the Saviour, in His goodness, to console and glorify her, now makes known.

"For she, in pouring this ointment upon my body, has done it for my burial."

Thy whole being, Mary, at this word, is shaken with sorrow and joy . . . Yes, thou art happy; for thy acts of love surpass all others, and the Saviour praises thee for them! Woman, by thy many and inimitable acts, thou hast honored thy Saviour most. But also what heart-rending view into the future is opened to thee! A few more days, and thy friend, thy God shall be seized by His enemies; thou shalt behold His adorable person, still impregnated with thy perfumes, covered with wounds and blood, and then taken away from thee entirely by the most cruel punishment of the cross.

Oh, that we, like Mary Magdalen, might profit of the fleeting hours, to honor Jesus! May we never forget that we belong to Him; that His body by the consecration returns to our altars, as to a cross, and, then, is locked up in the tabernacle as in a tomb, there to call forth and receive our generous homage. Who is more capable of offering it to Him than woman? Nor has she, from Mary Magdalen down, ever failed in this duty. In the newly born Church, women offered Jesus an asylum by receiving His Apostles or changing their mansions into sanctuaries, as did, at Rome, the Praxedes, the Pudentianas, the Priscillas, and Sabinas. It is woman still that to-day ornaments the altars, working with her hands gold and silk and precious tissues into beautiful vestments; she surrounds the Saviour in the tabernacle with lights and flowers and perfumes, and most assiduously watches at His feet. She gives Him of her wealth and even consecrates herself to Him in the touching roll of virgin, deaconess, or widow; or even, when married, loves Him with superhuman love and is ready at any time to undergo martyrdom, as did the Felicities and the Perpetuas. "It is something extremely touching," says Frederic Ozanam, "to see the respect with which the martyrs in prison treated those matrons of Christianity, our mothers in the faith, that set them the example and were for them, as it were, angels from Heaven; they had no wings, of course, but they had what angels lack, tears."

Since the primitive ages, generations of holy women have always flourished in the Church, and, in this regard, our century is in no way behind. Their number to-day is immense. Like the labors of the Church, theirs, too, embrace the earth, and keep on multiplying in a prodigious manner — all out of love to Him Who became their twofold Redeemer.

But Jesus is not satisfied with defending Mary against blame; He wishes to praise also and recompense her already here on earth. With the authority of Him Who commands the centuries, in the solemn form He employs in the assertion of the most important truths, the Saviour predicts:

"Amen, I say to you, wherever this Gospel shall be preached in the whole world, that also which she had done shall be told for a memory for her."

Behold, now, the former sinner associated with the glory of her Redeemer. The whole world shall re-echo her name. To the end of time, the most tender and loving hearts shall render her a cult of admiration and worship in the name of the Saviour, Who wished publicly to receive the last farewell of woman from her.

Mary, thy pardon dates but from yesterday; yet what care does not the Saviour take to give thee every chance of expressing thy love! How He is pleased to claim thee His own before the whole world!

# CLAUDIA PROCULA.

**WOMAN UPHOLDS JUSTICE.**

WE now have come to the saddest hour in the world's history: the Truth and the Justice is persecuted in the name of justice and truth; God is accused and condemned by men; the Messiah is to be put to death by those He came to save.

The princes of the priests and the doctors, the ancients, the Scribes, and the Pharisees, have succeeded in getting hold of Jesus by an armed mob. Bound with chains and ropes He is brought into the city of Jesusalem; their great council is assembled, and they condemn Him to death.

But will their judgment be confirmed? Will they obtain the permit for execution? Pilate,*) no doubt, will hold a personal enquiry, according to the forms of the Roman law; and, if he finds no ground for condemnation, may reverse the sentence.—His wife, too, may have prejudiced his views, since she belongs to the Judaizers.—What, if he heard favorable reports about Him?—What will the people do that loved Him, that had cheered Him as their prophet and the King of Israel? It was not impossible that Pilate would deliver Him out of their hands.

After the first interrogatory, the Sanhedrin is assembled, at an unusual hour, in the court of Gabbatha, before the house of the Pretor.**)

Pilate consents to open his court.***) The

---

*) Pontius Pilate was the sixth Roman governor, (A. D. 26—37) under the emperors Tiberius and Caligula. Philo represents him as haughty and obstinate.

**) There the Roman pretors held court. The name *pretorium* was also applied to the residence of the provincial government. During the Easter days, Pilate stayed at the castle Antonia, a fortified place, strong enough to resist any revolt and joined to a sumptuous palace. It was situated on the hill of Sion, north-east of the Temple, which, with all its enclosures and dependencies, was dominated by it.

***) Roman judges did not open court before the third hour, i. e., 9 o'clock A. M.

miracles attributed to Jesus, the Nazarean, His new doctrine, the life of His disciples, His many friends and enemies, all compel the Governor to hear this extraordinary case as soon as possible.

He even condescends to wait outside on the accusers, who, from religious scruples, did not want to enter the pretorium for fear of defilement. What do they ask? The confirmation of their sentence, the death of Jesus.

"What evil has He done?" asks the Governor. They bring forward vague accusations. Having re-entered the hall with his prisoner, he questions Him, and comes out again to tell them: "I find no guilt in Him."

"He is guilty of death," all cry, as with one voice.

Pilate is astonished and hesitates. But he has heard that Jesus is from Galilee and he thinks it best to send Him to Herod, the Governor of that province, who happens to be at Jerusalem for the Easter celebration. Vain hope! Herod, in his turn, sends back the prisoner. For a second time, the Saviour appears before Pilate, who begins another interrogatory, and again declares to His accusers:

"I find no cause in this man in those things wherein you accuse Him. No, nor Herod either."*) Futile efforts of a wavering will, of a weakness that increases the audacity of hatred.

Meanwhile, the crowd before the pretorium had swelled considerably. Pilate thinks an appeal to the people might be effective to deliver Jesus from the chiefs. "For upon the solemn day the Governor was accustomed to release to the people one prisoner, whom they would. And he had then a notorious prisoner called Barabbas. They, therefore, being gathered together, Pilate said: Whom will you that I release to you, Barabbas or Jesus?" And having said these words, he ascends the steps to the tribunal placed before the pretorium — a platform with a curulian chair. But the crowd, worked up by the chiefs, demands the release of the thief and murderer and the death of the Just. Not a man, not one in that multitude, rises in defense of the Saviour. Of all whom He had taught, consoled, cured, not one dares to plead His cause.

A woman alone, a heathen, at this hour,

---
*) Luke, XXIII. 14. seq.

called by Jesus "the hour of the powers of darkness", has the courage and the sense of justice to defend Him in spite of her own and her husband's material interests. She has a writing-tablet sent to Pilate whereon he reads: "Have you nothing to do with this just man. For I have suffered many things this day in a dream on account of Him." Claudia, the wife of the Governor, is not satisfied to think Jesus innocent and to give way to some sentimental feelings; she "suffers", and that less for her husband whose interests are menaced, than for "the just man" of the despised race of the Jews.

To suffer for the persecuted just, to suffer for a stranger, is contrary to all Roman ideas. Pilate is unable to make out the meaning.

But Claudia does even more than suffer for down-trodden innocence: she boldly pleads for it and intervenes with her husband. By nature woman is the help and counsel of man: God enlightens her for that purpose. "The inspirations even of a Christian are inferior to the sentiments of a woman. Women live with God far more than we; the reflex of His presence strikes them more promptly."*)

---

*) Louis Veuillot.

Claudia has an intuitive conviction, her sentiments are to be joined in with the judicial evidence of her husband. Together they are called to render the decision of the Roman and the heathen world upon the religious question.

Thus, in the beginning, Adam and Eve, in the name of humanity, had already decided that question; thus, in the course of time, both the intelligence of man and the heart of woman shall have to judge it. There can be no community of ideas and belief too great, no union of wills and mutual efforts of both sexes too powerful, to obtain the strength necessary to do one's duty.

According to the apocryphal gospel of Nicodemus, Pilate neither slights nor misunderstands the advice. He tells the Jews: "You know my wife honors God and judaizes with you?" — "Yes, we know it."*) But

---

*) According to the same gospel, Claudia, was a "proselyte of the gate", as all heathens were called who, without submitting to the Mosaic rite of formal introduction, renounced their idols and observed what is called the seven prescriptions of Noe. The name "proselyte of the gate" was an allusion to Exodus, XX. 10: "Thou shalt do no work on it (the Sabbath), neither thou . . . . . nor the stranger that is within thy

they add: "We have told you that He is a sorcerer, and by Beelzebub, the prince of the devils, He has the secret knowledge of all things. That is why He has sent this dream to your wife."

Alike to the rogues of all times, the Jews oppose but calumnies and pretexts. Yet their deft perfidies are unable to shake the conviction of the judge: the voice of his conscience, the message of his wife, the meekness and majesty of Jesus in the midst of falsehood and torture, His answers to his questions, all reveal to him a superior being and cause him perplexing anxiety . . . He re-ascends his tribunal with the firm resolution to release the accused. There, for the fifth time, he proclaims him "Just." But in vain. One more remedy he tries: scourging. But neither did that bloody sight appease the Saviour's implacable enemies. Fearful of losing Cesar's friendship, which meant his own office, the Governor finally hands Him over to them to be crucified.

The wretch! He no longer listens to the

---

gates." At this time so many Roman nobles became "proselytes of the gate" that the Roman Senate took rigorous measures against this religious movement. (Sepp, "Life of Jesus," vol. II.)

voice of justice or affection; he becomes a traitor to his conscience and the duty of his station, in order to remain governor. He will be governor a little longer, but Heaven and earth will make it known what crime he committed for that purpose.

And they will also tell what Claudia did for the Saviour and what she undertook to guard her husband against the weakness of his character and his ambition.

Christian women, wives of the chiefs and judges of the people, let us understand this woman and imitate her. Decisions are frequently given, votes are continuously cast, that concern religion, the clergy, the children, the honor and prosperity of the nation*): let us keep informed about them and see what we can do to guide them in the right

---

*) On this grave subject reproaches not less grave are directed against us, which we should not ignore. An eminent man, Jules Simon, in his work on "Woman in the XX. Century", blames the French women for not having resisted vigorously the laicization of the schools, the hospitals, and the administration of the government; of having been indifferent against the establishment of divorces, etc.; to which for the women of other countries may readily be added: indifference to the sanctity of Sundays and holidays, yellow journals, pornography, intemperance, etc.

direction; let us learn how to stand public calamities and the injustice done to the Church; how to diminish or remove the dangers to which, from all parts, the faithful, and especially youth, is exposed; let us instruct our own children and make them do their duty, in spite of public opinion and prevalent errors, in spite of the disgrace we may possibly incur from the powers that be...

Upon Claudia fell the task of defending right, justice and virtue at the pretorium. If she failed in preserving her husband from falling into the greatest crime ever committed, she at least performed her duty and made herself heard. If her pleading did not prevent the infamous sentence, it, nevertheless, increased his fears and remorses, and before God and the world she stands as an honorable woman who knew how to act and acted nobly.

It was for us that God willed this singular episode at the pretorium, and for our instruction the Spirit of the Lord moved the Evangelist to note this incident of the passion.

Claudia Procula belonged to the house of the Emperor Tiberius either by kinship or manumission. She afterwards became a

Christian, and, in all probability, she is the Claudia named by St. Paul in his epistle to Timothy and saluted by the Apostle as a friend.

The Oriental Church celebrates her feast October 27. under the title: Saint Procula, wife of Pilate.

# WOMEN ACCOMPANY JESUS TO CALVARY.

"HOSANNA to the Son of David! Blessed is He Who comes in the name of the Lord!" was the cry of the people of the city and the crowds of strangers that had flocked to Jerusalem for the celebration of the Passover. And the "Carpenter's Son" had made His triumphal entry over a carpet of leaves and flowers and vestments.

Five days later, covered with wounds and blood, crowned with thorns, and laden with a cross, the Triumpher marches to His execution through the same streets, accompanied by the vociferous clamor of the populace: "Crucify Him! Crucify Him!"

As God and man, as Saviour and victim, Jesus wished to receive from men such inconsistent treatment. It served both to establish brilliantly His divine and human nature, and to finish the work of Redemption. Up to His last days He had withdrawn from honors and homage; but then He sought it; up till then, He had lived to teach men by word and example; now He wants to atone for them. "His hour," the hour of our Redemption, has come.

The dreary cortège is formed: the centurion on horseback at the head of his cohort; next come the two robbers and Jesus, surrounded by the executioners and followed by the priests and ancients, Scribes and Pharisees, and an innumerable rabble. Only those that have witnessed the horrible sights of the Revolution can form a picture of this mob.

The evil inclinations and passions of the people, to which the hatred of the chiefs had appealed, show themselves in their whole ignoble violence, since they feel themselves protected and shielded by their superiors. It is a frightful spectacle, this populace with the eyes of wild beasts, their cries of fury, their cynicism and brutality towards the spotless Victim.

According to Roman custom, every malfactor sentenced to death, had to carry his own cross: thus Jesus carried His; he likewise carried the customary wooden tablet, on which his "crime" was written. Tormented by fever and thirst, bleeding still from the cruel scourging and crown of thorns, He bends under the heavy load, suffering agonies which alone the God-made-Man could enable nature to endure . . . Now He falls. The soldiers double their stripes and the populace its cries of hatred and vengeance!

An illustrious Catholic wrote in the days of his youth: "Had it been granted to us to live in the days of the Saviour and to pick out a moment in which to behold Him, we should have chosen that one in which, crowned with thorns and reeling and falling under the heavy cross, He marched to Calvary."*)

Since He had left Gethsemani, Jesus had been surrounded by persecutors only. Not a friendly word had been heard among all the injuries and stripes, not a glance of sympathy had He received in the midst of those ferocious looks of hatred.

---

*) The Count of Montalembert.

His disciples had fled; Peter had denied Him. Who shall show Him compassion?

The road from the hill of Sion to Golgatha is two Roman miles long. Continuing its march through the narrow streets of Jerusalem, the cortège followed the long road that leads to the Judicial gate, when, suddenly, a woman came forth from a house of splendid appearance and mixed up with the crowd. Her dignity imposed respect. With a resolute mien and the air of authority she forces a passage through the crowd of soldiers and executioners. Standing before Jesus, she wipes His face covered with spittle and dust and sweat and blood. And behold, the features of a dying God are traced indelibly on the napkin she had unfolded. It shall be a sublime souvenir of the Saviour's gratitude and of the agony He suffered at that moment of His bitter passion.

Oh heroic woman, take home thy treasure! It is not thine alone, but, thanks to thee, it belongs to the entire Church!*)

---

*) It is believed that the woman who performed this heroic act was Berenice, wife of Zacheus. Later on the name of Veronica — true image — was given her. According to tradition, Berenice took the napkin with the sacred image to Rome in the year 37. The galley,

## Women Accompany Jesus to Calvary.

According to the Talmud, the law forbade the shedding of tears, in fact, the manifestation of any sign of pity for a condemned man marching to his execution. Yet, there were still some other women that chose this moment to manifest their love and attachment for the Saviour of Israel. They follow His steps, weeping as if they were accompanying their first-born to the tomb. And they not only were privileged women that

---

which carried her over the sea, stopped at Zante. She profited by the occasion to preach Christ to the inhabitants. A great many heathens embraced the Christian faith, and the memory of Berenice is still alive at Zante. The pious woman is there the object of public veneration, and is looked upon as the first apostle of that place.

It is also told that, about the year 46, Zacheus and Berenice received from St. Peter the order to go to Gaul, but that, before leaving, Berenice confided her treasure to Clement, a disciple of Peter and his successor. An old chronique states: "At Rome is most carefully preserved the sacred napkin left to Pope Clement by the very pious Berenice, called by corruption Veronica, sister of Salome, niece of Herod the Great, and wife of the honorable Amadour." Amadour is the name under which Zacheus is still venerated in Aquitania.

The Bollandists confirm these facts: "Veronica arrived from the West in Soulac with St. Amadour." Having had the privilege of accompanying St. Martial on his missions, her memory is united with that of the

had enjoyed His intimate friendship, but there was a multitude "of women that bewailed and lamented Him."

Yes, women of Jerusalem, manifest your love, send forth your protest, harrass the criminals by your cries of indignation and sorrow! You accomplish, at this supreme hour, a necessary task, the most beautiful task, the eternal design of the Lord. You represent the religious soul of the nation, the

---

Apostle of Aquitania in all places evangelized by him, from Marseille to Soulac, where she died at the age of eighty-four, having spent twenty-three years in those holy labors.

The Church honors the memory of St. Veronica with maternal pride. One of the four mighty columns that sustain the cupola of St. Peter's, bears the name Veronica. It contains the miraculous napkin. Before the column, a majestic statue, the work of Bernini, represents Veronica unfolding the cloth on which the Saviour had just left the imprint of His Sacred Face.

The house of St. Veronica, on the Via Dolorosa, forms the fourth station of the Way of the Cross. For centuries it had been in the possession of the infidels and in a state of profanation, when, in spite of numerous difficulties and at a cost of considerable personal sacrifices, Mgr. Gregorios Youssef, Patriarch of the United Greeks, succeeded in acquiring it in 1884. Since then, free access to this holy place is assured to all pilgrims, and its restoration is begun. The church is dedicated to the Holy Face and the crypt to St. Veronica.

house of Jacob, the remnant of the house of Israel; you are the healthy part of humanity that marches in the fellowship of the Saviour and on whom the Spirit of Justice, of Light, and of Love has come to repose.

"Then Jesus turning to them, said: Daughters of Jerusalem, weep not over me, but weep for yourselves and for your children."

What a surprise! Jesus turns their eyes full of tears away from Him, to direct them upon themselves and their offspring and all the people He had come to save. "For if in the green wood they do these things, what shall be done in the dry?"

He is to die by the hands of men, such as are to be found at all times, the worst enemies of a truly religious nation, abusing law and authority, — and the people let them go! But every crime must have its punishment, and Jesus admonishes His own of the coming vengeance, that they may prepare and, at the first sign, flee from the city which has called down upon itself the blood of the Just.

Such is the goodness of Jesus that, in His most cruel sufferings, and at the very hour of His death, He thinks only of His elect and their welfare.

The women of Jerusalem give us a grand example that is worth remembering, although at that time their doings counted for little. Hence, the Gospel, so concise and pointed, tells us of the share they had in this greatest event of the world's history.

The Christian women of to-day have a role in life no less beautiful than that of the women accompanying Jesus to Calvary, if they wish to co-operate with the designs of divine Providence. More than one nation is led astray by its chiefs, who crucify the Saviour again, by denying His Church the right of existence and proscribing His doctrine. There, woman can save and build strongholds of faith in her own family; she can and must set the pace of morality. She can purify the moral atmosphere of the theaters and places of public amusement. If she refuses to go where virtue is ridiculed and vice exalted, the managers will soon change the tone of their productions. But alas! too many women find pleasure in lascivity; too many join in the cry: "Crucify Him! Crucify Him!"

Look down upon these, too, O Lord, and make them understand the value of their own souls and the souls of those they scandalize by their immoral conduct. Give them the tears of Mary Magdalen to weep over themselves and their sinful past!

# THE WOMEN ON GOLGATHA.

WE are on the hill of Golgatha. Three crosses are erected there. As if to indicate the greatest malfactor, Jesus hangs between the robbers. Foes and executioners and a crowd of curiosity-seekers surround Him. He alone attracts their eyes, as the object of their curiosity, or hatred. Upon whom will He rest His dying looks?

There are some women near Thy cross, O Jesus, grant to them this highest favor; for if men have blasphemed and crucified Thee, these women love and adore Thee.

Strong and generous hearts, women of manly courage, your Saviour desires to have you near Him in His last frightful agony. "Whilst but one man is there, three women, each called Mary, assist with their compassion, and sustain by their presence the dying Son of God: a virgin, a wife, a converted public sinner, — in a word, woman as she is found in all conditions on earth. Who does not see here a living symbol and, as it were, a practical prophecy, of the role woman is destined to play in the Christian Church? They stand at the foot of the Cross, unshaken in their faith, immutable in their love, and merciful and courageous in their assistance to the Saviour, Who is but too often abandoned by men."*)

At this dire completion of the work of Redemption, woman, indeed, had to be present, to protest against the crime of the deicide nation; to repare the fault of Eve, and unite in atonement with the Saviour by personal affliction; she had to be there, to be, by the divine Blood, consecrated to the new life, to which the doctrine, the example, and the special call of the Master had invited her.

Woman, there on thy reconquered place,

---

\*) Abbé Charles Perraud.

thou first shalt receive the baptism of Redemption and learn the grand lesson: There is no salvation without suffering.

"Now there stood by the Cross of Jesus, His mother, and His mother's sister, Mary of Cleophas, and Mary Magdalen."*)

The mother beholds her Son crucified,— such a mother, such a Son. Yet the "Woman of type and prophecy", the Virgin hailed by the angel and blessed by all generations, is also to be the *Mother of Sorrows.* "And thy own soul a sword shall pierce."**) Poor Mother, thou hast seen thy Son deliver Himself to His executioners with infinite meekness; thou hast seen Him stretch out His hands and feet upon the ignominious cross; thou hast seen these crude and coarse nails, and, height of horrors! thou hast heard the hammering that drove them through His august members; thou hast felt the shock He received, when recklessly the cross was planted into the earth, already drenched by His blood; thou hast undergone all this, O Mother, and the end is not yet. For three endless hours this great Victim in His rack-

---

*) John, XIX. 25.
**) Luke, II. 35.

ing, writhing agony, is to be before thy eyes. His pangs are thine; yet, when death has ended His, thine are renewed by the aspect of His torn and mangled body.

Mary, standing by the Cross, shared all her Son's sufferings. By woman death had come into the world; by woman we received life again. By means of her consent to this divine sacrifice, she became, as it were, the co-redemptrix of the human race, its second mother.

Jesus knew and felt her suffering, and forgetful of His own, sought to alleviate hers. "When therefore, Jesus had seen His mother and the disciple standing, whom He loved, He saith to His mother: Woman behold thy son!"

With infinite tenderness and compassion He addresses these words to her: "Woman (second Eve), behold thy son!" What a reward for John's faithful love! The mother of Jesus is to be his own mother, and he, the brother of Jesus! Can it be? To confirm the bequest to his astonished disciple, Jesus repeats it, saying: "Behold thy mother!" Love her, honor her, care for her! But not to John alone is Mary given as mother; as "the

Woman", the second Eve, the mother of life, at this solemn hour, she becomes the mother of us all!

Tenderest love had spoken these words, but for a moment they increased the pangs of Mary's heart. What an exchange! The disciple, although the best beloved, is given for the Master; the son of Zebedee for the Son of God! Yet that same childlike humility that prompted her to submit to the angel's message in the Incarnation, now makes her repeat the words: "Be it done to me according to Thy word."

After these bequests of filial love, and a last look at His sorrowful mother, Jesus has no more earthly cares, He turns to His Father. That moment in the work of Redemption has arrived, when the supreme relations between Heaven and earth are established. A few more seconds, and the hour shall strike that the centuries hear and adore, the hour constantly reverberating in the decrees of eternity, the hour of deliverance and pardon, the hour of the world's resurrection, the hour forever blessed, but also forever cursed, the hour of scandal, the hour of darkness, the hour of consummated deicide!

"Jesus bows His head and gives up the ghost."

All are "sore afraid" and flee, whilst you alone, O women, stay to watch over the body of your Crucified Love. You are in your proper place there, representing womankind of every age, guarding in her soul, protecting against His enemies, the God Whom the Jews have killed. Sad and silent you linger. What will happen next? is the question that increases your anxiety. Will the Governor, contrary to all law, allow the embalming of the body and an honorable burial? Will not the hatred of the Jews interfere again?

Whilst they are thus in suspense, the soldiers approach and finish the two robbers by breaking their bones; but seeing that Jesus was already dead, one of them "with a spear opened His side, and immediately there came out blood and water."—"Having loved His own... He loved them unto the end."*) The last drop of His precious blood is to be shed for our Redemption.

You, holy women, who have shared the sufferings of the Divine Victim, atoning for

---
*) John, XIII. 1.

the sins of the world, and also felt their sweetness, you now will know how to convince especially your own sex, what a signal favor it is to suffer with Jesus near His Cross; you will be able to explain to them that sacrifice is not alone a religious, but also a human and a social law, that it is at once a power and a glory.

But now, "Virgins of Sion", your cruel waiting comes to an end. The Governor has given the body to Joseph. Jesus is to be taken from the cross. Cast a last glance at this "King of the Jews", always beautiful, even now, in the pallor of death. His head reposes on His bloody chest with a serenity and glory that infinitely surpass the celestial beauties which brighten the death of the just.

Approach, women of Calvary, gather your forces to sustain this august body that Joseph of Arimathea and Nicodemus let down with tenderest care. This body, all bruised and mangled, delicate and trembling arms will receive it. All centuries have seen thee, and all centuries will see thee, o Virgin, Mother of Sorrows, holding in thy arms the pallid body of thy Son! Sublime scene, that the greatest geniuses with all their talent have tried to paint, but of which each and all have given but a faint sketch.

One more sacrifice is asked of thee, sorrowful Mother: thou must separate even from the corpse of thy Son; it must be embalmed and buried, and thou must live without it.

The funeral cortège takes the road to the garden of Joseph, in which there is a new sepulchre. "And the women that were come with Him from Galilee, followed after, saw the sepulchre, and how His body was laid."*)

As long as they can, they stay around the tomb, but a moment comes where love and attachment are checked by the impossible. Such is the present moment. And if your hearts should break, you will have to leave the beloved dead, and walk back to Jerusalem without Him. But rejoice: as you are consecrated to Him by sorrow, which is the Redeemer's ointment, you, hereafter, shall live with Him in a mystic, yet no less intimate and real manner, and you shall communicate this life to others at the cenaculum in Jerusalem. Providence itself will guide you to that religious and social life to which the Saviour invited you.

---
*) Luke, XXIII. 55.

# MARY MAGDALEN AT THE TOMB OF JESUS.

GOLGATHA hill is deserted and silent. The shadows of evening surround it. The crowds of the curious and perfidious Jews, the soldiers and executioners have returned to the city. Joseph of Arimathea and Nicodemus, too, have left the sepulchre and have reached their home. In Jerusalem has subsided the clamor of the day on which the Messiah was executed.

But two women linger in the garden of Joseph, near the sepulchre of Jesus. Absorbed by woeful emotions, they do not see that evening begins to cast its dark veil over the mystery of a God Who died for men.

Mary Magdalen and the other Mary are sitting there, in front of the sepulchre, immovable and downcast, unwilling to separate from the tomb of the adored Saviour. But night approaches; they, too, must return to Jerusalem to observe the Sabbath.

Sorrows and tears increase with the silence and the darkness. Mary of Magdala passes the night in suffering. When it finally dawns, it is but the beginning of a day that confirms the reality of the Saviour's death and His loss forever!

"And when the Sabbath was passed and the first day of the week began, Mary Magdalen, and Mary the mother of James, and Salome bought sweet spices, that coming they might anoint Jesus."*)

To get back near the body of Jesus, to surround it with the most delicate attentions, to behold it again, and remain near it was what their love desired, although it could be but a weak consolation for so deep a sorrow.

Hasten, then Mary, for the princes of the priests and the Pharisees have likewise come to inspect the tomb of their victim; they have sealed it and set a watch around it. Both

---

*) Mark, XVI. 1.

hatred and love everlastingly watch near the Saviour.

Night comes once more with its dreary solitude and the same mental anguish, but this night, too, finally passes. Mary can restrain herself no longer; whilst it is still dark, she hastens through the streets of Jerusalem towards the sepulchre. "And on the first day in the week, Mary Magdalen cometh early, when it was yet dark unto the sepulchre: and she saw the stone taken away from the sepulchre."*) A horrible suspicion rises within her: have they profaned the tomb? And in her fright, she runs to tell Peter and the other disciple, whom Jesus loved: "They have taken away the Lord out of the sepulchre, and we do not know where they have laid Him." Both hastened to the sepulchre, inspected it, and found "the linen cloth lying, and the napkin that had been about His head not lying with the linen cloth, but apart, rapt up into one place.... they saw all, and departed again for their home."

Yes, these men, these Apostles, the future head of the Church and John, the disciple, loving and beloved, know nothing better

---
*) John, XX. 1—18.

than to return home.... Not so Mary. He is not here anymore, where is He? That is what torments her, what causes her agony. Forsaken again by those who could and should have helped her, with a mind darkened by sorrow, what can she do to find the body of her adorable Lord?

Such is the anxiety of a soul that, having felt God's presence and tasted His sweetness, finds itself bereft of it. It suffers, and nothing in Heaven and earth can satisfy its craving.

"But Mary stood at the sepulchre without, weeping." To long for God, and to seek Him, brings Him near. Magdalen, who, in spite of the contempt of the guests and the bickering of Judas, had persisted in honoring the Saviour at the Pharisee's banquet, who, despite the hatred of the judges, had followed Him to Calvary; who had stood by when His disciples fled and Heaven itself seemed to be shut against Him; who had come to the sepulchre morning and evening; who had loved so much and now, in His death, mourns the loss of her all and weeps bitterly;—she is to be the first to see the Saviour arisen, before any other women, even before the Apostles.

Jesus, however, makes Himself known by degrees only.

"Now as she was weeping, she stooped down and looked into the sepulchre: and she saw two angels in white, sitting one at the head, and one at the feet where the body had lain. They say to her: Woman, why weepest thou? She saith to them: Because they have taken away my Lord: and I know not where they have laid Him."

Ye Christian souls that weep, behold what happens, and do not despair! Your angel will come to your rescue also; he will suggest cheerful thoughts, he will bring about the unexpected, he will direct some helping hand towards you. Mary already enters upon the road of consolation: she is led out of her sorrows. Is it not a privilege to be questioned by angels, the guardians of the Lord? Will she not learn some news about her God's disappearance? However, she does not recognize them, she does not understand the happy news that the Saviour's day of triumph over death has dawned. Thus misery often prevents us from feeling the help God has already sent us. Yet what Mary saw were real angels; why is she sightbound?

All at once, she hears something behind her. She looks up. No doubt, that is the gardener. He says to her: "Woman, why weepest thou? Whom seekest thou?" What, Lord, dost Thou not know whom she is seeking? Thou dost; but to instruct us and to soothe her, she shall repeat it and once more breathe forth her love and sorrow. She replied: "Sir, if thou hast taken Him hence, tell me where thou hast laid Him: and I will take Him away."

Darkness disappears, angels and secrets vanish; Jesus reveals Himself. For it was He. "Mary!" says He. "Teacher!" cries she. One word from each—that is enough—one word to understand and answer each other! In spite of all the graces granted, the soul often stays in doubt; but when it hears the voice of God, so distinct from all other voices, it hesitates no longer.

Word of God, speak to our soul in its affliction, speak to it, and it will fly to Thee as the center of its life. Word of God, aid us not only by Thy angels and their inspirations, by Thy priests and their instructions, by Thy sacraments and their consolations, by the events that, in slow wisdom, Thy Providence disposes: come to our aid directly, speak but one word, O Jesus, one single word, and we shall be comforted! Thus "Jesus, rising early the first day of the week, appeared first to Mary Magdalen, out of whom He had cast seven devils," but who, since, had loved Him more than all the rest.

Acting the role of all souls that suffer, because God, Whom they knew and Whom they loved, is in hiding, Mary Magdalen represents also those that suffer, seeking the unknown God and the truth of religion.....

Let them seek! Let them pray! Let them wait! Sooner or later they shall have their angels, their advisers, their decisive events and, finally, their Easter-morning, where God Himself will dry their tears, by showing Himself to them.

"Teacher", Mary Magdalen said. That one word shows her relation to the Saviour, the most beautiful, the most ennobling, the most touching relation, the relation of pupil to teacher, of ward to tutor — a relation of reverence, of loving devotion, and gratitude. Who can describe her happiness? Apparently she can not cease kissing the feet of the Saviour, the more so as she fears to lose Him again. For His appearance was no longer earthly. Hence He said to her: "Do not touch me (any longer), for I am not yet ascended to my Father: but go to my brethren, and say to them: I ascend to my Father and to your Father, to my God and to your God." He did not prevent her from embracing His feet in the outburst of her joy, but He tells her it must come to an end; she shall see Him again on other occassions; not yet is He gone to Heaven; nor can He go at once; a most important work is to be completed first—the foundation of His Church—and she shall help in the work. Therefore, she is to go now and tell His brethren: "I ascend to my Father and to your Father, to my God and to your God."

Such is the trying duty of Thy friends, O Jesus; having found Thee after much agony, they have to quit Thee again and go to work. But we may rest assured of happiness. We work for the Lord, that Lord, Who, despite the crimes of earth, delights in being with the children of men and being one of them; for even now in His state of glory He calls them His brethren: declaring thereby that all men by divine adoption shall become children of God and, thus, His brethren. Such is the aim of God's prodigal love and our highest destiny.

Jesus addressed these words to a woman, a former public sinner. Mary is charged with announcing His glorious resurrection and to confirm the divine adoption.

Elated with joy over the vision, she hastens to tell the disciples, who are all downcast: "I have seen the Lord and these things He said to me." But nothing can persuade them, neither her most ardent assertions, nor her exuberant happiness, nor those words that could proceed but from the heart of Him Who had given them so many proofs of His love.

Their obstinate incredulity resists. Who knows, but in their eyes she is still the sinful woman? They never understood the pardon of the Saviour nor the heroism of that nature. They are still vulgar-minded and full of cowardice.

But what does it matter? Mary has fulfilled her mission: they may believe or not, she has seen and she has heard the Master!

If at times we zealously endeavor to lead sinners back to God, to inspire them with love for Christ, let us not be surprised by the coldness and indifference we meet with; let us not even wonder at any contempt or hostility we may encounter. Happy in the possession of truth and having done our duty, we may let time and circumstances, let God Himself, do the rest. When we consider with what contempt Mary was treated since her conversion, how much distrust and unfriendliness she had to bear; when we recall what doubts must have saddened her on her return to the sepulchre,—we shall be glad to submit to a similar treatment; for as sure as the Gospel has announced to the world what Mary did at the house of Simon and at the sepulchre to honor the Saviour, so Heaven will publish eternally what we have done to honor the Saviour in His churches, in teaching Him to His brethren, in defending Him before the world; and the labors we endure, the rebuffs and insults we suffer for His sake, shall be as many jewels in our crown of immortality.

# THE HOLY WOMEN AT THE SEPULCHRE OF JESUS.

N Golgatha the holy women had seen the Saviour bow His head and give up His ghost, they had felt His cold body; then they had wrapt it in white linens,—as they imagined, never again to be unwrapt. Sadness preys upon them: He Whom they love, is no more. Not a thought strikes them of the possibility of His resurrection, not one remembers His promise and prophecy.

Not even Mary Magdalen, initiated more deeply than others into the mysteries of His life and death by her symbolic unctions, has understood, or else she has completely forgotten, the words of the Master. His enemies, though, have not forgotten them. Carefully they had noted them, and now the princes of the priests and Pharisees stand before Pilate, telling him: "Sir, we have remembered that that seducer said while He was alive yet: After three days I will rise again. Command therefore the sepulchre to be guarded until the third day."*)

Jesus, Thy enemies are still afraid of Thee, in spite of their victory. They have torn Thee and nailed Thee to the cross; they have seen Thee buried, and yet they are not satisfied; they feel restless and uneasy. "Let His body be watched," — as if to say: He is alive still.

This fear shall henceforth be the lot of all the Saviour's enemies. His foes of to-day are afraid even of His likeness. The crucifix must be removed from the eyes of the children at school, from the view of jurors and judges in the court room, and, in the hospitals, out of the reach of the dying, lest they, by kissing the wounds of the crucified Redeemer, may feel at ease in their last hour by the renewed hope in God's mercy.

Crucified God, there is no longer room for

---

*) Matt., XXVII. 62—66.

Thee on the walls where our forefathers placed Thee. To the world of to-day Thy aspect is as troublesome as it was at the time of Pilate.

But if these women have forgotten the promises of the Saviour, they have not forgotten their duty toward the dead body of their Master, now resting in His tomb. Whilst, after the embalming, Mary Magdalen stayed in meditation near it, the other women hastened to Jerusalem to purchase spices with which to cover the body in the tomb. But one thought is in their minds: the hasty work of this evening must be done over. No time is to be lost. The sun has already disappeared from the horizon, and the stars begin to twinkle. In a few minutes each family will be assembled, and the torches will be lit to eat the Paschal lamb. No one as yet knows that the figure has been replaced by the reality, the Paschal lamb by the Lamb of God, immolated on Mount Calvary. The friends of Jesus pass these hours in silent seclusion; depressing perplexities and cruel anxiety weigh upon them. The night seems endless; so does the festival day following it, despite its pomp, its sacrifices and its religious canticles. The Mosaic rites but add to their gloom, and the legal ceremonies cannot allay their anguish nor quiet their impatience to be again near the tomb of their Crucified Love.

No sooner is the Sabbath over than Mary of Cleophas and Salome set out to buy spices and to prepare everything for the embalming of the body of Jesus the next morning. They and their companions are animated by the same thought.

But what were the disciples of Jesus doing whilst these women, to the best of their ability, were busy honoring Him? Some had left Jerusalem, like Thomas; others were in hiding, or shut up in the Cenaculum for fear of the Jews; all were apprehensive and inactive. What a contrast between them and these women! Yet glaring as the contrast already is, we soon shall see it widen still more.

Early in the morning, the women march in groups to the sepulchre; the first of them arrive there before sunrise; soon they are all gathered around the tomb of Him Whom they served so faithfully during His life.

But "who shall roll us back the stone from the door of the sepulchre?" they say to one another. They knew their combined strength would be unable to lift it. Undismayed, they arrive at the tomb, and, lo! the stone is rolled back; and entering into the sepulchre, to their still greater astonishment, they do not find the body of Jesus, but a young man dressed in white, who tells them: "Be not affrighted, you seek Jesus of Nazareth Who was crucified: He is risen, He is not here; behold the place where they had laid Him."

The angel re-assured, consoled, and instructed them: "Behold," he said, "the place where they had laid Him;" verify it now for yourselves, in order to make certain the resurrection of the Saviour, which is the foundation of your faith. The religion of Jesus must rest on personal and profound conviction, and we must adhere to it of our own free will. On this day of the Lord's resurrection, women above all are called to a clear understanding. Their zeal deserved it. They were the first at the tomb, as if there was nothing of greater importance. And really, hereafter, nothing will be of greater import either to themselves or to the Church, whose deft and generous help they shall be. Taught thus by the angel, they receive a glorious message: "Go, tell His disciples and Peter that He is risen."

A real apostolate is the reward given to women for their zeal on behalf of the Saviour while alive, and their fidelity to Him in His death: "Tell the disciples and Peter!" Is this not a correct outline of the union between laymen and priests for the spread of the Gospel, a true delineation of the hierarchic and harmonious duality within the Christian apostolate? In the Church, all shall speak of God, all have to be about the heavenly Father's business, both the faithful people and their pastors: the former with regard to one another, following their leaders within just limits, at times taking even the initiative of the Saints to aid, instruct, and excite those clad with pastoral authority; as the holy women, who, by order of the Saviour, informed their superiors of His resurrection, caused two of them, Peter and John, to visit the sepulchre, and made known to them all that they were to see Him in Galilee and that He was to ascend into Heaven.

Every one has a charge with regard to his neighbor; every one must exert some personal influence upon others. Without the subordinate assistance of all, the sacred ministry can reach but few souls. It frequently has need itself of being encouraged and stimulated to further activity by the zeal of the faithful. How weak did not the Church in France become, when the Christian people, without any outside works, confined themselves to walk sleepily in the old beaten paths! On the contrary, what vigor has it developed since noble and courageous impulses aid the zeal of the priesthood!

It is the Spirit that quickens the body of the Church; He, according to His own choice, suggests to laymen [*] or priests new works, which, when approved by proper authority and adapted to the living body of the Church, blossom and yield fruit in abundance.

The priesthood has not necessarily a monopoly of such inspirations. Faith is not to be imprisoned in the soul of any one, nor is charity to shrink into a sentiment; but faith is to spread and charity to act. Who cares but for himself is nothing; *Christian individualism* so-called is ultimately destruc-

---

[*] Ozanam, Montalembert, Windthorst, Garcia Moreno, the foundresses of the Propagation of Faith, and many others, are striking examples.

tive of the true Christian charity, whose aim is to distribute all real goods, both of soul and body; to spread them continuously in all directions, knowing no bounds except those set by the laws of the Church's constitution.

Let, therefore, everyone be an apostle, not sentimentally, but practically, that all may learn from his words and example. Let each take an interest in, and help, all public and social works that aim to bring about a more equitable distribution of the goods of this earth. Thus each shall announce to his brethren the risen Saviour, Who is the Redeemer of the bodily, earthly, no less than of the spiritual, heavenly life. And let nothing stand in our way: neither distaste for daily routine, nor sloth, nor the hatred of the ungodly. The women of the Gospel have risen above the mockeries of the vulgar, above the judgment of the judges, above the scandal of the zealots, above the ban of the Synagogue. They remain true to their now glorified Saviour and the mission they received from Him at the sepulchre.

Timid still of heart, but elated in mind, they hasten to announce the joyous tidings to the Apostles. On the road, unexpectedly, Jesus meets them, saying:

"All hail! But they came up and took hold of His feet, and adored Him. And Jesus saith to them: Fear not. Go, tell my brethren that they go into Galilee, there they shall see me."*)

The good work intended by the pious women had already merited for them the news of Christ's resurrection; their eagerness to publish it deserved a confirmation. By working for God, faith increases, charity develops; but by lukewarmness and sloth the apostolate usually ends by seeing its own certitude vanish. Do good, and you will come to light, is a true word and continuously verified.

The holy women, strengthened by this evidence, arise in haste to announce to the disciples that the Saviour is risen. On this occasion, they go as apostles to the Apostles to announce to them the fact upon which hinges our religion. They go to tell them that they are still the friends, the brethren of the Saviour, and that it is their duty to make it known to all, that all are brethren, members of the same family—the Church of Christ.

---
*) Matt., XXVIII. 8—10.

Thy brethren, Lord?..... Thy love makes Thee forget the sufferings and tortures men have inflicted upon Thee. No matter: Thou art a member of the human family.... Thy Apostles, the chosen ones of Thy love, have abandoned Thee—that, too, is forgotten and forgiven—they are always Thy brethren.

And Thou chargest Thy sisters to tell them. O Lord, what a word! "Go, tell my brethren." What a word is this, pronounced at the moment of Thy resurrection, at a time where Thy whole being belongs no longer to earth, but to Heaven. Thus Thou dost re-aver, Thou, the God of meekness and of pardon, that Thou art always our brother. Truly, Thou art our brother, but no one knew this brotherhood; Thou hast brought it down from Heaven into this world. Men use it now as a weapon against Thee, yet what other word proceeded from Thy heart that is more touching and more plainly manifests Thy love? Jesus, show Thyself once more to this world, that does not know Thee any more. Thou alone canst save it. Thou alone canst wean it from so many false fraternities that gull it out of Thy true brotherhood. Show Thyself also to Thy disciples and to Thy friends, that they may know Thee better and be more than ever convinced that, even after having offended Thee so often, and having separated so frequently from Thee, nay, after having denied Thee for a time, they have nothing to fear, but have only to come back to Thy love to be received most graciously.

The Saviour has vanished. The holy women hasten to Jerusalem. "What will be the surprise of the Apostles! Will they not, when they hear the glad tidings, leap with joy and with us adore the Saviour, now glorious and triumphant?" Such thoughts passed through their minds, but, alas! Returning from the sepulchre, "they told all these things to the Eleven, and to all the rest. And it was Mary Magdalen, and Joanna, and Mary of James, and the other women that were with them, who told these things to the Apostles. And these words seemed to them idle tales, and they did not believe them."[*]

Their good news does not bring joy, as they had expected. A mocking and incredulous smile and hurting words are the first and apparently only result of the message,— the thrilling message of the resurrection, which they were so eager to announce.

---
[*] Luke, XXIV. 9—11.

Christian women, this story is repeated daily. Often your loving devotion meets with cold apathy, your living faith provokes but deadly sarcasm. Does it surprise you? The holy women met with these trying dispositions in the Apostles on the radiant day of the Saviour's resurrection. Even at this memorable juncture man showed himself, as he did and does but too often, an absolute enemy of himself. To believe would be the end of his sorrow, would fill his breast with joy; but he refuses.

Know, then, how to wait. Soon the disciples will go to the sepulchre, soon the Saviour will show Himself to their incredulity also, and convince them. And should we pronounce the name of the Saviour for no other purpose but to rescue it from oblivion, we would perform a precious work. What we sow by our hand, God must make it germ. Our work may be hard, and, in appearance, fruitless; but, after the example of the holy women, let us not be dismayed. Within the family and beyond, let us continue to scatter in all directions, into the souls of all our brethren, that eminently saving word: Christ is risen!

# THE WOMEN AT THE CENACULUM.

THE Sacrifice of Golgatha is finished; the work of our Redemption is completed. Immense treasures of grace are stored up, awaiting distribution and application to the souls of men. The seed which the Saviour brought into the world and fructified with his own blood is to be scattered over the earth to grow and yield fruit in the soul of every rational creature.

To prepare His disciples for this task, Jesus, at His Ascension, commanded them not to depart from Jerusalem, but to await the coming of the Holy Ghost. Mindful of this command, they stayed together in an upper room of a house belonging to Joseph of Arimathea, situated on Mount Sion, near the ruins of David's palace and the burial place of the kings. That hall had already been hallowed by the institution of the Holy Eucharist, whence it is called up to the present day the "Cenaculum," the "supper room." There, too, in frequent visits, the glorified Saviour had freed the minds of His disciples from the illusion, that the Messiah was to be an earthly ruler or political liberator of His people, and had filled their hearts with a great longing for the Paraclete.

Confiding in the promise of the Saviour, they waited for the baptism of the Holy Ghost. United with them were the holy women who had been so fervent at the Saviour's tomb and so eager to bear His message. The Apostles ceded to them the place which they had hitherto occupied near the Saviour, no longer keeping them separate, as was the Jewish custom, in the Temple and the synagogues. They all prayed together in union with Mary, the Mother of Jesus. From the beginning of Christianity the prayer of the Virgin was what it is to-day, a maternal help, a perfume of love, that penetrates the hearts and disposes them for the coming of the Holy Ghost. "And all these were persevering in prayer with the women, and Mary, the Mother of Jesus, and His brethren."*) And when the days of Pentecost were accomplished, they were all together in one place:

"And suddenly there came a sound from Heaven as of a mighty wind coming, and it filled the whole house where they were sitting. And there appeared to them parted tongues, as it were of fire, and it sat upon every one of them. And they were all filled with the Holy Ghost, and they began to speak divers tongues, according as the Holy Ghost gave them to speak."

"All were filled with the Holy Ghost," hence the women also. Tradition tells us that the fulness of the Holy Ghost descended on the Mother of Jesus, and that from her, in the shape of fiery tongues, it spread over each of those present, as if to show that the divine Mother, surrounded by the Apostles, who are the strength of the Church, is the soul thereof, and their common queen.

---

*) Acts, I—II.

O Virgin of the prophets, full of grace, your presence in this august assembly was to consummate the communion of the faithful in the unity of the Holy Ghost, and to let the liberating grace and truth of the Redemption shed its lustre upon all mankind. Queen of Heaven and earth, type of purity and moral beauty, you hold there the place of honor, to introduce your sex to the new era of liberty and apostleship.

The admission of women to that holy reunion, on the day of Pentecost, meant the upsetting of universal custom, the end of the old world. Birth is given to a new society, in which woman shall play a roll worthy of her sanctified soul. Woman, — she whom Jesus had healed and instructed, pardoned and elevated, consoled and enlightened, — is exteriorly and finally consecrated and destined for the sanctification of earth and the vision of Heaven. She, too, is called to share in establishing the reign of truth.

The prophet Joel had predicted it: "And it shall come to pass after this, that I will pour out my spirit upon all flesh: and your sons and your daughters shall prophesy: your old men shall dream dreams, and your young men shall see visions. Moreover, upon my servants and handmaids in those days I will pour forth my spirit."*)

That is to say: I shall give to my servant-maids and to my daughters the understanding of the word of God, that they may practice and teach it the same as do my servants and sons. Thus, besides having her personal position in the family circle restored, woman is also given an important place in society. By the will of the Redeemer, she is not only to recover all rights of personality and human dignity, but she is also to be associated in the work of the Redemption.

"I recommend to you Phoebe, our sister, who is in the ministry of the Church," writes St. Paul to the Romans, "that you receive her in the Lord, as it becometh Saints: and that you assist her in whatsoever business she shall have need of you. For she also assisted many, and myself also."

"Salute Prisca and Aquilla, my helpers in Christ Jesus."

And the Apostle also sends greeting to his brethren and his sisters, co-operators in his mission: Mary, Persis, Priscilla, Julia, and the mother of Rufus, whom he calls his own.

---
*) Joel, II. 28—29.

As in Palestine at the time of the Saviour, so later at Rome, women became the best auxiliaries of the Apostles. Apostles themselves, and instituted deaconesses to fulfill certain functions with women, especially in the administration of baptism, they have a large share in the rapid spread of holy faith.

The first Christian women of Rome came principally from the lower classes of society, but soon divers Patricians joined them. For Christianity, from its start, embraced both the ignorant and the learned, the poor and the rich.

Priscilla and her husband, Cornelius Pudens, opened their palace on the Viminal to the Apostle St. Peter. Pomponia Graecina, a matron of the highest rank, wife of the consul Plautius, buried the body of the Apostle in the Vatican crypt, the property of her family, and that of St. Paul in a tomb on the Ostian road. Her grandchild Plautilla, the disciple and friend of St. Paul, had the religious zeal of her grand-mother: she was one of the first Christian virgins. Neither is Ania Faustina, the wife of Antoninus, afraid to join the "hated sect," nor Praxedes and Pudentiana, daughters of Cornelius

Pudens, whose palace on the Viminal became the cradle of Christianity at Rome and the privileged place where Pius I. established the baptismal font. Caecilia converts her husband Valerian and her brother-in-law, Tiburtius, as also those whom the Prefect Almachius had sent for their execution. They were baptized in her palace by Pope Urban. "Father," she says to him, "I have asked this delay from the Lord, to place into your hands these poor, whom I feed, this house, that shall be consecrated a church forever."

Among the great Christian women of that time, our sisters in the faith, let us also name Susanna, daughter of the Senator Gabinius, whose knowledge equaled her beauty, and whom Diocletian wanted to give in marriage to the Emperor Maximinian. She perished amid tortures, together with others, whom she had gained over to the Saviour. The same day on which she was "born for heaven," Pope Cajus consecrated her palace into a church and celebrated there the holy mysteries.

Next we behold the Empress Severa, wife of Diocletian, and her daughter, Valeria, regenerated in baptism. Eutropia, wife of Maximinian Hercules, disposes her son-in-law, Constantine, in favor of the Christian religion. Of Greek origin, she as well as her daughter Fausta, possessed Grecian beauty and intelligence; her charms and her zeal made her triumph over the new Caesar. Constantia, his sister, joins in her efforts, and both gain Constantine over to the faith, as also his mother, the Empress Helena.

The favorable edict of Milan (A. D. 328), by which liberty was granted to the Christian religion, was due to the constant labors of the Roman pontiffs, but likewise to the incessant and persuasive efforts of these admirable Christian women.

They continued their apostolate by erecting churches to the true God. The Empress Fausta built one near her sumptuous dwelling on the Lateran, and Constantia, another in honor of St. Agnes.

To restore the profaned holy places in Palestine, Helena erected there churches in honor of the Holy Cross, of the Ascension, and of the Nativity at Bethlehem. At the age of 85, she undertook the dangerous voyage to Palestine: "Let us go without delay," she said, "to venerate the places where the feet of the Saviour touched the earth." And, when there, she went in search of the Cross, saying: "We are at the place of the execution, but where is the sign of our Redemption? What, shall I rule, and the Cross of the Saviour be lying in the dust? How can I believe myself saved, if I do not see the sign of my Redemption?"

Patrician ladies, too, quit their splendid dwellings on the Aventine. "I will establish my abode," said St. Paula, "where my Saviour had His, and the fatherland of my God shall also be my resting place." And she took up her abode at Bethlehem.

In the Orient, St. Pulcheria, the granddaughter of the great Theodosius and heir of his genius, at the age of sixteen, teaching her brother, exhibited such proofs of wisdom that, in 415, the title of Augusta was conferred upon her. Her zeal against the heresies of Nestorius and Eutyches evoked the praise of St. Leo: "You were never found wanting to the priesthood and the Christian faith. In the name and the authority of the Blessed Apostle St. Peter, I constitute you my special legate to conduct this affair before the Emperor."

In 450, Valentinian III. arrives at Rome with his mother Placidia and his wife Eudoxia. Pope St. Leo conjures them to come to the rescue of the endangered faith. Three years later, Placidia, on her death bed, recommends the maintenance of the true faith in the East, and of the poor, her heirs.

In the next century, Constantina, the wife of the Emperor Mauritius, and Theotista, her sister, gave considerable sums from their personal property for the assistance and ransom of Christians, and rendered the most faithful help to the Sovereign Pontiff.

Pope Gregory the Great addresses himself directly to Leontia, the wife of the cruel Phocas, to follow the example of Placidia and Helena in defending the Church. Under the same pontificate, Theolinda, daughter of Garibald, duke of Bavaria, and wife of the Lombard King Autharis, converts Agiluf, whom she married later on, after the death of her first husband. A picture by Matthew Bader represents her as teaching the mystery of the most holy Trinity.

To Theolinda, Gregory the Great dedicated his dialogues, of which she made use in converting the Lombards; to her he also addressed his last letter. When, in 615, she had become tutor of her son and regent of the kingdom, she cleared away the last vestiges of Arianism and idolatry, built churches and monasteries, instructed the people and fostered the sciences.

At this period of turmoil, war was incessantly waged between the nations of the old world. In spite of all, the spirit of the Cenaculum spread even among the barbarians. Under pressure from the Goths and Vandals, the Gallo-Romans and Burgundians, later on the Germans and Franks, fulfill a most fruitful mission.

Clothilde completes the conversion of Clovis, and with it, that of the Franks, an event of vast importance. By Clothilde a mutual understanding is also brought about between the clergy and the King.

Radegundis, so grand and touching in her misfortunes, Radegundis, learned and the friend of the learned, takes care of the poor at the royal palace of Asties, turning it into a hospital. "When the lepers, coming to the Queen, uncovered themselves at a given signal, the servant maid enquired whence they came and took their number. After that they were bid to come in; the table was spread for them, wine and cups set on it. St. Radegundis personally waited on the women infected with leprosy, embraced and kissed them, and loved them with all her heart in God. Then she washed their faces with warm water, anointed their hands, nails and ulcers, and served them at table. When they were dismissed, her royal generosity did not fail to make them presents of gold or vestments, all in secret, her trusty servant maid alone knowing about it. The famous monastery of the Holy Cross, at the gates of Poitiers, was built by her on her domain."

In Spain, Indegundis and Riguntha, of the Merowingian race, became the apostles of faith, the latter by the conversion of her husband Reccared, who became the founder of the Christian monarchy, and, with his wife, assisted at the Council of Toledo.

The first to preach the faith among the Anglo-Saxons is Bertha, who would not consent to marry Ethelbert, king of Kent, unless he allowed her full liberty in the practice of her religion. When this consent was given, she disposed Ethelbert so well that he received favorably Augustin and his forty monk companions, sent by Gregory the Great to evangelize England. This same Pope writes to her: "We praise the Almighty, Who has deigned to reserve for you the conversion of the English nation, as He made use of the glorious Helena, mother of Constantine, to direct the hearts of the Romans towards the Christian faith."

Since then, Great Britain has won fame by the number of its saints. Nowhere can an equal number of women be found so distinguished by birth and virtue, that founded monasteries and shut themselves up within them, after forming themselves to a religious life in the abbeys of Chelles, Jouarre and Faremoutiers. The most famous among them are Hilda, Ebba, and Etheldreda, Mildreda, and her sisters, all princesses of royal blood. The first founded two monasteries and, for thirty years, governed them with great wisdom. In those days the authority of abbesses in Anglo-Saxon countries was almost equal to that of bishops and abbots. They negotiated public affairs with kings and princes, and frequently assisted at national assemblies.

Friedeswieda founded a monastery, that became the cradle of Oxford University, and Cuthburga established Winbourne, held in great renown by the religious and learned men at a time when the Abbesses Tetta and Lioba had five hundred nuns under their jurisdiction.

Like their sisters of the Cenaculum, they, too, had received the spirit of the apostleship, which moved them to leave their country, and their beloved monasteries, to further the labors of the first apostles of Germany.

"God speed you," said St. Aldhelm to them; "you are the flowers of the Church, the pearls of Christ, the heirs of his heavenly kingdom; but you are also my sisters in the monastic life, and my pupils by the lessons I have given you. God bless you, valiant and courageous virgins, watch, persevere, triumph in your holy undertaking."

Besides religious virtues, manual labor, the study of the sciences, Greek and Latin, were favorite pursuits in the cloisters of Thuringia, Bavaria, and Frankonia, all peopled by those admirable Benedictine nuns.

In 852, Oda, a Frankonian princess, wife of Ludolf, Duke of Saxony, erected the famous monastery of Gandersheim. Its Abbess, a hundred years later, was Gerberge, daughter of the Duke of Bavaria, endowed with the most brilliant talents. With her passionate love for studies she inspired the young Hrotswitha, a dramatical poetess and oratrix, who was far ahead of her times.

Another famous abbess was St. Hildegardis, who wielded a powerful influence over her contemporaries. Nothing is more interesting than her correspondence with popes, emperors and princes, secular and regular clergymen.

In the following century, St. Gertrudis unites to her aureola of sanctity the laurels of learning. As humble of heart as she was gifted in intellect, she was for forty years the servant of her sisterhood.

Let us name also Hedwig, wife of Henry, Duke of Silesia and Poland, whose virtues are so brilliantly reflected in her niece, St. Elizabeth of Hungary. As the apostle of her country, she trains her subjects in truth, justice, and peace. Her courage equals her zeal. She delivers her husband from captivity and repels the invasion of the Tartars. Pierced by the deepest sorrow at the death of her son Henry, she exclaims: "My God, I thank Thee for having made me the mother of a son who knew how to die the death of a martyr for his religion and his country."

In Bulgaria, Prince Bogoris received the light of faith from his sister. In baptism he took the name of Michael and desired all his people likewise to be counted among the children of God.

In Russia, religion made little headway until the conversion of the princess Olga, whose grandchild Wladimir and with him the whole nation received baptism in 987.

In the troublesome times of the struggle between the papacy and the empire, it is again a woman that becomes the type of devotion and attachment to the Church, — the Countess Mathilda, daughter of Boniface, Markgrave and Duke of Toscany. She loved the Church with a most filial love, and with the Church her beautiful Italy. To defend both she empties her treasury, raises armies, and fights at their head; though beaten at times, she is never discouraged, and avenges herself by more signal victories. Always faithful to Gregory VII., she is also his confidante, his ally, and his defender. After his death, her adherence to the papacy is unshaken, and, having fought for Urban II. against her cousin, the hypocritical and audacious adversary of the Popes, she died in 1115, leaving to the Holy See her vast possessions as the last pledge of her love for the Church, whose independence she desired to secure, because she believed the independence of the Church closely bound up with that of Italy. A great number of slaves belonging to her domain, were set free. At the hour of her death, she kissed with tender emotion the Crucifix and prayed: "O Thou Whom I have served so much, serve me now."

"With Mathilda," writes the chaplain of Canossa, "the honor and glory of Italy descended into the tomb."

Later on, two women, Catharine and Brigitta, one of most humble birth, the daughter of a dyer in Siena, named Benincasa, the other of princely descent, powerfully served the Church and all Christendom. Catharine of Siena and Brigitta of Sweden persuade

Gregory XI. to leave Avignon, for 70 years the residence of the popes, to go back to Rome. Catharine combats public scandals, pacifies Italy, and in all things is the counselor and support of the papacy. Urban VI. calls her to Rome to co-operate in the salvation of souls and the re-establishment of Italian unity.

"Lord," she prayed, "if Thy justice demands absolute satisfaction, do not reject the prayer and the offering of Thy servant-maid. Behold me ready to undergo the punishment due Thy people. For the glory of Thy name I shall willingly empty the cup of suffering and death. Such has been my heart's desire since the day I consecrated myself to Thee."

Brigitta was the daughter of Birger Person and was related to the Swedish sovereign. June 14, 1303, was born this child, "whose voice shall be heard by the entire world," as the Blessed Virgin had revealed to Benedict, curate of Findal.

By the will of her father, she was married to Wulfon, Prince of Nericia. Wulfon, returning from a pilgrimage to St. James in Gallicia, fell dangerously sick at Arras. At the instant prayers of Brigitta, St. Denis, the patron-saint of France, assured her of his recovery. In gratitude thereof Wulfon entered a monastery where he died shortly afterwards.

At the court of Magnus, to which she, by the will of God, returned in her widowhood, she obtained from the King needed reforms for her country and fought incessantly in defense of the people.

But her great mission, like that of St. Catharine of Siena, was the reform of the Church and Christendom by bringing the Pope back to Rome.

Into Lithuania the Christian religion was introduced by the marriage of King Jagello with St. Hedwig in 1386. The King was baptized, and at the assembly of the grandees the Christian faith was declared to be henceforth the religion of the State.

Endless is this royal chronology. Volumes could be filled with the names alone of these heroines of the first centuries and the Middle Ages, that, coming from among all classes of people and of all nationalities, exercised the apostolate of Christ.

This divine mission was never interrupted. Everywhere and always, at the cost of the greatest sacrifices, women have shown their devotion and zeal for the salvation of souls, as did their sisters of the Cenaculum.

During the reign of Terror in France, many examples of undaunted courage are recorded among women, among young girls, and modest servant-maids. Not only did women give shelter to priests, but they penetrated into the very prisons, carrying thither, besides religious consolation, also material assistance. By means especially of little girls, incarcerated priests were enabled to receive Holy Communion.

In 1795, Susanna Loyant had herself locked up with the prisoners the night before their execution, to exhort them and help them to make an act of perfect contrition, because no priest could be had to hear their confessions. Miss Loyant died the death of a Saint in 1836 at Laval.

In our days, too, if many women have become strangers to religion, or its outspoken enemies, others, and that a great number, aid the successors of the Apostles in bringing back these stray sheep to the fold and participate in every good work and in all generous efforts, aiming at the good of religion and society. Women should, above all, rally the friends of justice and progress, should work for pacification in the midst of the divisions and antagonisms that disturb society. In early Anglo-Saxon poetry it is said of woman, that she weaves the bonds of peace. More than ever in our days, should she weave the bonds of peace between all upright and sincere souls. Nothing would be more powerful now than such a spirit of peace and concord as reigned at the Cenaculum between the disciples of our Lord. They called themselves "brethren" and served one another as such. "Men-brethren," and "Women-sisters," say the Apostles to the newly baptized in the Spirit. They help one another, instruct one another, even push their union so far as to share with one another their wordly possessions, by a spontaneous and voluntary sacrifice, inspired by the teaching of Jesus and the Spirit of divine love. "Who lives in light shall love in fire."

"Do you not know," says St. Paul, "that you are the temple of God and the Holy Ghost dwells in you?" Too few know it in reality. The wonderful gifts of grace do not captivate all that are baptized and believe. But a few elect, like those of the Cenaculum, live by this indwelling grace and make it daily more dominant in their love-brightened souls.

Let us march onward, then, as our mothers in the faith, filling the world with virtue and by it with more genuine happiness. With all our might, let us call upon the eternal Spirit of the Father and the Son, unceasingly descending from the heights of glory. The feast of Pentecost is to-day, and shall be to-morrow, in the perpetual union of souls in the Holy Spirit.

DEO GRATIAS.

www.ingramcontent.com/pod-product-compliance
Lightning Source LLC
Chambersburg PA
CBHW031745230426
43669CB00007B/487